The Island of Macromol

The Birth, Life, and Decay of Innovation

The Island of Macromol

The Birth, Life, and Decay of Innovation

By Michael C. Geoghegan

First Printing: 2015
Second Printing: 2019

ISBN 978-1-329-07216-9

TABLE OF CONTENTS

PREFACE

Death vs. Regeneration: A Scientific and Social Explanation of Corporations

The journey of Gullivan in THE ISLAND OF MACROMOL is based
on the career of an individual, trained as a Ph.D. chemist and MBA, who
arrives at a huge, successful multi-national company in the 1960s. He sees
how collective corporate intelligence has exploited macromolecular chemistry
for vast profit across a range of decades and businesses. His contributions
earn him the position of research fellow, inviting him to chart his own course,
giving him time for future-casting that is outside the boundaries of thinking
and behaviors that had built the company up to that time.

From this open space of reflection and his unique history, Gullivan studies
the relationship between the corporation's products and the evolution of
the market. As a result, he is able to predict the coming death of certain
businesses and he sets about trying to communicate to the management what
he sees so clearly. Yet this proves impossible, even over a long period, though it
is not clear why. He cannot fathom how such smart and successful people can
be so reluctant or unaware or simply unable to hear what is being said.

Instead they continue to make bad investments, even as he predicts they will
be bad and explains to them in advance why they will fail. As a consequence,
he finds himself unwittingly cast in the role of court jester, able to "speak truth
to power" but still unable to move either the rational or the social levers of
change. Rather than becoming passive and settling for his sinecure, he pushes
further until he formulates an explanatory model of why a previously successful
business would want to create such insurmountable obstacles to change.

THE ISLAND OF MACROMOL delivers a unique synthesis, a rigorous
argument and a prescriptive approach to making good business decisions
by design. In rejecting the accepted wisdom of the MBA curriculum and
drawing core concepts from a selected range of sciences and social theory,

Gullivan creates a larger framework for understanding processes of innovation and for ensuring good investments. The story is clear and compelling.

From thermodynamics comes the process of "making order out of disorder." Taking natural resources out of the ground to manufacture materials is one example. Organizing newer ideas from prior ideas is the same process – organizing new and useful semantic structures, procedures, or instructions, through invention of new language. In the course of natural selection, new distinctions arise and create opportunity to define new actions, which in turn bring about change.

In all cases this is the technical meaning of "work" and work creates value. This is the foundation of every business. What come new from Gullivan are techniques for measuring the economic potential of a given or proposed business, in order to decide what scale of investment is warranted by projected future profits. Thus he answers the question of what makes a good investment, as well as its corollary, whether there should be investment at all, even in a current business that seems to be sailing along profitably.

A smartly-run business uses its earnings to make improvements in its operations, creating a surplus out of surplus. But the environment of a successful business is bound to evolve. Every business must have the capacity to see this evolution and to react to it as necessary to maintain its viability. Yet human systems are by nature conservative and resistant to change, even in the face of declining profits and apparent disaster ahead. Again, this is no surprise, for the long list of previously successful businesses that fail is huge compared to the stories of businesses lasting 100 years.

What is surprising is the cause of this conservatism, the barricade against change. It is not that the business sees the nature of the market evolution and decides it is not a threat. The surprise is that the internal social system – specifically its language – is *incapable of seeing* the external change. The old language of the corporation – the same language that enabled it to become focused, effective and successful – becomes its downfall. The same efficiency of language that leads to success, as Gullivan witnessed, is a form of rigidity, of inability to evolve, of death.

And so, the question came begging, can this be prevented – under what circumstances may an organization regenerate itself? Herein also lies the question of where innovation comes from and its answer comes from human social behavior and cybernetics.

If an organization's inability to evolve is the old language that structures the truth, what process can be undertaken to invent new language, new truth? First, whatever the process is to be, it must be protected from the natural resistance that comes from the self-interest of the existing social system, from the executives and managers whose identity is invested in today's money-making processes. The delicate and uncertain process of gestating new language for future business cannot compete with the demands of time and attention made by today's business. Gestating new language needs a protected mechanism with its own resources, which Gullivan dubs "The Queen." This metaphor is not meant to conjure a single individual but to contrast with the forces of "The Prince," who rules the current business and is focused on further conquest of the known. In contrast, The Queen is interested in procreation, that is, the recombination of genes – in the form of ideas or memes – that lead to new language. This new language is able to "see" the evolving environment in a way that opens a new semantic space of opportunity, of wealth creation.

Now, what gene pool is to be drawn from? Is the company's internal pool of memes enough to create a new space of economic possibilities? Likely not, but this must be determined from the cybernetics of conversation. Learning, problem framing, trust and collaboration all arise from conversation, necessary precursors to bringing forth new language. In addition to the social nature of conversation, there is the crucial concept of "requisite variety" – the capabilities and capacities of a system to achieve its goals. A core contribution of the discipline of cybernetics, this concept had previously been interpreted only in physical systems. To understand the conditions on Macromol, and therefore all organizations that cannot get out of their own way, Gullivan creatively adapts requisite variety to apply to the social system of an organization – to define the necessary and sufficient systemic capacity of a conversation to create new value through new language.

The organizational mechanism of the Queen – whether an individual or group or committee – does not hold these conversations herself. Rather the Queen nurtures the genetic mutation of ideas for the creation of new language, new memes that can pervade the thinking, and therefore the actions, of the organization – should they deserve to. In the search for formulating and solving problems in the evolving environment, these new memes are observed to be effective or not, and the Queen then feeds, that is, selects and gives resources to, the offspring that show promise in their infancy. Over time the privileged offspring mature and grow in capacity from a small-scale "focusing" problem to eventually encompass an entire new business.

Thus, Gullivan's journey braids the nature of work, wealth, conversation and variety. But we must also be aware of personal motivation and self-interest, whether of the executive who stands in the way of losing power or the worker who needs clarity of her role to collaborate effectively toward shared business goals. Gullivan's motivation and the impetus behind his quest is a personal empathy for those who lose their careers in the "transition" from a dying corporation to a more successful one, usually expressed with the euphemism, "creative destruction of capital." Through the discipline of a scientist, and the time and genius to reflect upon, question, and supersede accepted wisdom, he provides a roadmap for "creative conservation of capital."

This book is about the source of technological and social change, the necessary and sufficient conditions to harness that source, and the inevitable resistance to change by the now-successful. Fortunately, it also offers remedies.

Paul Pangaro
New York City
2013

BOOK I

ACQUIRING A POINT OF VIEW

It is not the answer that enlightens, but the question. – Ionesco

A few winters ago, Gullivan left an island he called Macromol. Gullivan had been there for over 30 years without knowing it. In fact, much to his surprise, he did not realize that he had been so absorbed in the affairs of Macromol until he left the island. It dawned on him later, after he had wandered into new places, explored new spaces and engaged in new conversations that, in time, he had come to realize that the island of Macromol was no ordinary island – it was a place of special conversations, different from the sea of conversations which surrounded it. Macromol was an island ruled by a Prince surrounded by a small group of Cardinals and a somewhat larger group of Courtiers. The main activities in the island were carried out by four tribes, each with its own chief: the Technicals, the Persuaders, the Makers and the Counters, and some specialists such as lawyers and "personnel directors." Sometimes the tribal boundaries were blurred inasmuch as there were some inhabitants who could be viewed as the Technical dealers or Technical makers. The inhabitants of the island were busy making a living through creating, making and exporting all manner of string.

During his time on Macromol, Gullivan began to notice that there were more inhabitants leaving the island than new people were arriving, and the trend seemed to be accelerating with time. He wondered why this "depopulation" was occurring. He noticed also that the flow of new products, new items of consumption, had slowed down. Perhaps the investments that were being made in Research and Development were no longer as fruitful as they had been in the past. Hence he became puzzled by a question – what, indeed, is a good investment? How does one recognize, select and amplify a good investment? As a child, Gullivan was aware of and, indeed, excited by the wonder of what he later came to know as an investment and the investment process.

He remembered how building a new barn on the farm or getting the first tractor had transformed the lives of all around; how it brought a new sense of hope, an elevated energy, a view of the future which looked bright and exciting. These investments were generative, created surpluses that were reinvested in the farm, and life expanded. In later years, Gullivan realized personally the consequences of bad decisions, bad investments and the resulting waste of capital. He saw how bad investments led to decay, destruction and despair and, indeed, the death of hope. Gullivan saw how investment decisions had deep social consequences.

Gullivan was not especially interested in the day-to-day ongoing problems of life in Macromol or on other islands in their infancy or adolescence and their particular investment decisions. He began trying to solve the puzzle of how to recognize a good investment using the language of finance. The approach was not satisfying as it lacked rigor and was subject to wishful thinking. Being a scientist, he turned to thermodynamics – the language of work, heat, order, and disorder. In that language, he found a system of explanations that satisfied his need for rigor and predictability. This confidence in thermodynamics, however, raised an even deeper puzzle – if a good investment can be recognized and selected, why was it that the investors in Macromol consistently made bad investments and rejected what seemed to be good investments? This second puzzle engaged him for over a decade before he found a satisfactory set of explanations. While in Macromol, he learned new languages, the languages of evolutionary and developmental biology and of language itself. He engaged in new conversations about the nature of the nervous system, the biology of language, how purpose arises, and about the politics and historical nature of self-interest. He came to the conclusion that in successful, or previously successful, old populations, new conversations seldom arose. Those conversations, which he would classify as evolutionarily current in new social domains, beyond those old populations, are by and large unnatural to the previously successful old population. Recognizing that all investments are preceded by agreements, and that these agreements are reached through conversation, he realized that the solution to his puzzle lay in understanding why these new conversations could not take place within those old populations. This story is about the journey he took to find answers to why this is so. Let me begin the tale at the time young Gullivan began to acquire a point of view, when his curiosity was aroused.

The Acquisition of a Point of View — "Who was that Man on the Bus?"

We arrive in time with no thoughts,
no language, no beliefs, and begin our journey.

It was a beautiful day when young Gullivan walked down the long avenue, under the massive evergreen oaks, on his way to school. The year was 1945. He was eight years old. As he caught the 44A bus on his way to St. Canices School, he was thinking of the May altar he had decorated the night before. The daffodils, the blue bells, the red current blossoms and the candles, it was the month of the Virgin Mary. At Castle Avenue, a tall, lean, dark-haired man got on the bus and took a seat in the back. Gullivan was sitting on a side seat still thinking about the altar when they looked at each other. The man had large dark rimmed glasses, a lean face and sat unusually erect. He looked at Gullivan with a mixture of intensity, interest and softness. Gullivan looked away, and then back again, wondering who this man was, what he was thinking about.

Gullivan got off the bus at his usual stop and, as he walked the rest of the way to school, he kept thinking about the man and how different he was from anyone he had encountered before. During the next week, Gullivan saw him again several times on the bus, and his curiosity continued to grow. Then he was gone and Gullivan never saw him again.

A few years later, Gullivan left the Christian Brothers at Canices and went to a boarding school at Garbally, Balinasloe, County Galway. There he was introduced to the wonders of science and the joys of rugby. He did well in school, both academically and athletically, and especially on the rugby field. During the long summer vacations, he worked on the family "farm" surrounding their large Georgian mansion. There were extensive woods, a stream at the edge of the property, and a classic 12-foot walled English-style garden, a full acre in size. The garden had three large greenhouses, a wide variety of apples, pears, plums, figs, berries and vegetables of many kinds. Gullivan spent many hours exploring the gardens, the eleven acres around the house and the hundreds of acres of the old St. Ann's estate, which was just beyond the back field.

There were eleven in his family, four brothers and four sisters. Gullivan was the seventh. They played many games together – hurling, football, tennis, hide and seek, and on Sunday nights, cards, usually "110." Gullivan was always curious about nature and spent many hours watching the tadpoles in the stream or climbing trees to see the birds hatching their young. At one time he had a large collection of bird eggs. At other times he assisted Jack, their extraordinarily versatile handyman, in building barns and sheds, soldering the old lead pipes and pruning the fruit trees. He learned a great deal from Jack: gardening, carpentry, metal work, and how to go about such tasks.

In 1955 Gullivan entered the University College Dublin, Faculty of Science. The first few years there were relatively easy and again his interests were divided between science and the rugby field. The subjects grew more complicated in his fourth year, when he was introduced to thermodynamics and quantum physics. He had an American professor for the latter subject. In his first lecture, the professor told him that quantum physics was quite different from classical physics. He suggested that we read through all three textbooks without trying to make sense of everything, page by page, the first time. Then he said read them all again, and indeed, for a third time. Then the professor said read them for comprehension, since after three cursory readings you should have acquired some sense of what this strange subject was about, and you should be in a position to converse in detail. The professor also noted that many of these questions that arise early on will be resolved later as you gain understanding. So Gullivan developed a dim understanding of the Schrödinger wave equation, and at the same time, a new appreciation for how to learn an entirely new subject. In his fourth year at University, he had learned how to learn a new and difficult subject. While studying quantum mechanics, Gullivan came across a photograph of Schrödinger.

The man on the bus was indeed Ernest Schrödinger himself.

At a later time, Gullivan read his book on *What is Life* and was profoundly influenced by his style of thinking. For example, Schrödinger deduced from basic physics the necessary and sufficient properties DNA must have in order to carry out its function of "information" storage and transfer. DNA had to be an aperiodic crystal.

After Gullivan's fourth year honors exam, he was interested in continuing on to do a Ph.D. in chemistry. He knew he did not want to be a practicing chemist, but was interested in learning how to do research. Gullivan still remembers the puzzled look on the professor's face when he discussed his purpose with him. For the first two years, his research project on mechanisms in flavonoid chemistry seemed to go nowhere. At many of the periodic research group discussion sessions, he had nothing to report and was convinced that his project would never bear fruit. Then, within a period of about two months, he had a break-through and discovered some twenty new compounds, and developed an understanding of his special branch of chemistry. Shortly after that the professor told him to write up his thesis. In 1963, Sir Christopher Ingold examined his work. He passed the oral examination and was awarded his Ph.D.

In December of 1963, Gullivan arrived in New York City. He was now 26 years old and was excited to be in a new land. He had arranged for a post-doctoral position at Columbia University and, in the course of his research there, he met Pat Moran. Pat had heard that Gullivan was a rugby player and invited him to join the Old Blue Rugby Club. This was Gullivan's first real introduction to American life and the beginning of a life-long association with the "Old Blues." In addition to his post-doctoral work, Gullivan was curious about how the business world worked, so he also enrolled in the business school at Columbia and received an MBA degree. In 1966, he left New York for Delaware, for the Island of Macromol, where he started his first real paid job. Despite the geographic separation, he never left the Old Blues.

On his train journey from New York to Delaware, Gullivan wondered why his chance encounter with Erwin Schrödinger had made such a deep impression on him many years ago. Why did he still remember it so well? He was puzzled and it would be many years later, perhaps when he read Alan Watts' book, *On the Way of Zen*, that he began to understand the intuitive mind, direct experience and why the talking mind has limitations, and, indeed, often gets in the way when trying to solve complex problems. Perhaps that's why Einstein became the beam of light, embodied light, to see time and space as it is – of course in a thought experiment.

1. Out of clutter, find simplicity

2. From discord, find harmony.

3. In the middle of difficulty lies opportunity.

– Three Rules of Work, Albert Einstein

BOOK II

EARLY TALES IN MACROMOL

Understanding begins by not accepting the world as it appears.

When Gullivan arrived in the island of Macromol in the late 60's, it was the epicenter of the world of chemistry. In Gullivan's early days there, he was often unsure and apprehensive. It seemed everyone he met was very bright, particularly in the technical arena. Many people were world-class in their fields and exuded much confidence about what they were doing. He joined a small group working on new elastic strings. During his second year on the island, a great debate ensued between the Technicals and the Persuaders about how to price a new, very fine elastic string. Gullivan took great interest in this question, and, reflecting on what he had learned at Columbia Business School, asked himself "What do I need to know in order to solve this problem?" So back to physics – using Hooke's law for elastic materials, he established a general relationship between the specific physical properties of the string (e.g. stress/strain) and its practical value in everyday use. This provided a basis for pricing all classes of elastic string. At that time, pricing by engineering principles was quite radical.

From elastic string Gullivan moved on to help solve problems associated with special strings used to make mats. Among the many technical and manufacturing challenges in this new area, one was formative for Gullivan. For a number of years much effort had been focused on developing an effective anti-static system for mats. The Technicals had developed a string with a conductive carbon core, which, in principle, should dissipate any electrostatic charge buildup, and hence, should eliminate the chance of getting a shock while walking on the mat in a dry environment. However, the conductive string did not work according to predictions. Gullivan managed the mat testing and evaluation group at that time and was puzzled by this failure. He posed to the group the question, "What has to happen in order that the system will not work as planned?" He also asked, "How could we recognize and predict success?" The Technical Chief, an amateur radio enthusiast, authoritatively asserted the prevailing wisdom, that the mechanism of action was that of conduction (just like the car battery). Gullivan was not a physicist, but the theory did not seem right to him. He went back to his old physics books and finally hypothesized that the mechanism of action was inductive (like an alternator) rather than conductive, and that this hypothesis could explain the observed test results. His group designed a series of experiments to validate the inductive hypothesis, but the results, even though they had included all the variables thought to be relevant, did not provide clear-cut answers. Gullivan persevered, under the assumption they had missed a key parameter in the tests. That turned out to be the case. In a few days, with a few key changes, a new theory in action, they confirmed the inductive mechanism and began one of the most successful new product launches in the history of the mat string business.

This experience led Gullivan to question, in general, underlying "theory" or assumptions that give rise to the so-called facts. The wrong theory in this case gave rise to fallacious facts, to strongly held views, and to many man-years of fruitless research and development.

Shortly after that, Gullivan asked a young physicist to work out the physics of the mechanisms by which the mats got dirty. She did an outstanding job and provided the theoretical basis for many new products in this area. Along the way, the basic science that underlay this work tended to get lost, as new Technicals got involved in anti-dirt/soiling product development programs. From this experience Gullivan learned that when a new inhabitant was assigned to product development in an area in which there was considerable past experience, that past experience was ignored. It often seemed that the new inhabitant did not review the old work, as is usually the case in research. Perhaps reinventing the wheel made sense in the context of job security: solving the problem was not the most important issue, having a "good project" was.

During Gullivan's first ten years on Macromol, he got to know many businesses well. Teams formed naturally around business problems in all areas and across all "boundaries." Teams often included people from all tribes: Technicals, Makers, Persuaders, Counters and the Courtiers. Problems once identified were discussed in fully represented "venture committees" and were dealt with on sensible business basis. It was the age of management by objectives and it seemed that both business opportunities and personal career development were boundless. Gullivan read much of the significant management literature, as did others, and there were many discussions about its usefulness. However, as time passed, it seemed to Gullivan that the old familiar rigorous technical and business discussions were being displaced by more abstract ideas such as theory X versus theory Y, the role of management, and organization theory. A host of new courses appeared on such general subjects as writing, listening, career development and "brain style." The list grew on and on.

Around 1977, Gullivan's Chief decided it was time for him to change assignments. Gullivan was offered a job in the newly formed Feedstock Division of Central Research and Development. This was a professional position – a move away from the diffuse accountability and the somewhat protected position of a Manager, to a job with a highly visible relationship between personal contribution and performance evaluation. The Feedstock group was populated almost exclusively by Technicals who had a great deal of reverence for the "numbers." These Technicals had sophisticated computer programs for evaluating the cost of producing oil, in particular oil from shale. Gullivan learned a great deal about the economics of oil, coal, and natural gas production. He also studied the dynamics of U.S. energy demand over the decades since World War II. He did not feel that all the massive computational analysis was very relevant to predicting future energy prices. The Middle East, after all, had vast known resources of oil, and future prices of energy should reflect the quality and abundance of energy, and of course, geopolitical factors, GNP, productivity growth, oil/gas finding rates, increases in demand, and energy use productivity. Gullivan concluded that oil prices were going to fall over the next few years. This was contrary to the prevailing wisdom among members of the group and its management, and indeed, of representatives from major oil companies who visited Macromol. Gullivan felt completely out of place. He discovered the economist office held a view similar to his, but it was not publicly shared.

After a difficult year, Gullivan left the Feedstock group and returned to manage a technical product development group in new types of string. Shortly after that, he got a call from the manager in the string planning group. He offered Gullivan a job with an unusual challenge – "Tell us what is going on in the world, what is going to happen over the next 20 years and how is that going to affect the global business of man-made string?" Gullivan accepted the assignment and began a journey along a wholly different path. He left the security of operations where what to do tomorrow flows transparently from what is going on today. Rather than being asked to come up with the answers, he was faced with the problem of posing the questions. It was 1979 and was his last direct assignment in Macromol. For the next 20 years Gullivan had to chart his own course.

Where are we going over the next 20 years?

To see where you are going, look behind you.

This type of problem was new to Gullivan and he spent many days in his office staring out the window, wondering where to start and how to proceed with the task. He had been used to solving tangible, discussable problems where one could run experiments to confirm that one was moving in the right direction. He began to read available futures studies, e.g. the Club of Rome work, and the U.S. Project 2000 sponsored by Jimmy Carter. The most useful study was "Interfutures: Facing the Future," a study done under the auspices of OECD and sponsored by the Japanese government. This study contained an historical data analysis of all of the developed economies and most of the important developing economies. A scenario approach was used to make assumptions explicit, to assess interactions of these assumptions and to explain the interactive consequences of explicit governmental strategies or guidelines in such areas as energy, trade, industry redeployment, foreign investment, monetary policy, etc. This formidable piece of work – done by very competent people from around the world – he read many times, but felt he was missing an organizing principle or principles by which he might collapse much of the complexity and give him some guidance as to which scenarios or combinations of scenarios were more probable. He decided to let go of all the data and analysis and look elsewhere. He remembered his introduction to quantum mechanics many years ago.

During the next six-month period, he had nothing to report and was feeling very uncomfortable. The entire subject seemed to be getting more complex and confusing, diverging rather than making sense to him. He asked himself – was he really doing anything useful? Making any progress? He started to read extensively outside the futures areas, beginning with Aristotle, Adam Smith, Darwin, following his intuitions about where he might find something illuminating. Gullivan read Schumpeter's work and was struck by the following passage:

> *First, since we are dealing with a process whose every element takes considerable time in revealing its true features and ultimate effects, there is no point to appraising the performance of that process ex visu of a given point of time: we must judge its performance over time, as it unfolds through decades or centuries. A system – any system, economic or other – that at every given point of time fully utilizes its possibilities to the best advantage may yet in the long run be inferior to a system that does so at no given point of time, because the latter's failure to do so may be a condition for the level or speed of long-run performance...*

> *...The usual theorist's paper and the usual government commission's report practically never try to see that behavior, on the one hand, as a result of a piece of past history and, on the other hand, as an attempt to deal with a situation that is sure to change presently – as an attempt by those firms to keep on their feet, on ground that is slipping away from under them. In other words, the problem that is usually being visualized is how capitalism administers existing structures, whereas the relevant problem is how it creates and destroys them. As long as this is not recognized, the investigator does a meaningless job. As soon as it is recognized, his outlook on capitalist practice and its social results changes considerably.*

So, Gullivan decided to go back and review some history, particularly the history of ideas, what people thought, what they think now, what is the truth now. What is going on in the world of ideas? It seemed to Gullivan that at any point or period in history there are theories or central ideas that pervade many or perhaps all disciplines of thought or inquiry. Consider for example, the development and expansion of Newtonian "logic" in the 18th century. The universe was a clock-work mechanism so we had the age of mechanisms, cause and effect. The dominant methodology of explaining by both scientists and philosophers was indicative. Following the claims of Bacon, Locke and Newton, the "thinkers" were convinced that the only way to true under-standing and explanation was through induction, inference from observable facts to simple generalizations. However, as advances were made in the understanding of electricity, heat theory (thermodynamics), pneumatics, chemistry, and physiology, many felt it was time to change the norms of science and philosophic inquiry itself, to find a new way to theorize about unseen entities. This led to the hypothetical deductive methodology, i.e., to start with the theory and then deduce what must be so. By the end of the 19th century, this new approach was pervasive in physics, biology and philosophy.

The theory organized the data. The breakaway from the tyranny of mechanism, proximal cause and effect had begun. The powerful belief in objectivity began to loosen its grip. In the early 20th century, Niels Bohr had introduced the complementary principle: the perceived mode of an atomic entity depends on the experimental arrangement in use, i.e., we see what we measure, and indeed, a major problem in physics was that every word in the language refers to our ordinary perceptions; you cannot separate physics from the physicist. At the same time, Heisenberg stated that the more precise the electron's position is known, the less precise can its momentum be ascertained.

This made us aware of fundamental and intrinsic unknowability, and indeed, as we specialize, the more our knowledge deepens in one discipline, the more our ignorance grows in other areas. Similar changes in ways of looking at the world were occurring in art: Cezanne with multiple perspectives, Schönberg with atonal music, Joyce with the inner subjective narrative. Heidegger, the German philosopher, claimed that "objectiveness" emerges from the background, or context, when there is a breakdown or a problem that causes us to pay attention, and of course, we all see problems in our own way. These metaphors also showed up in Freud's ideas on mental illness, or wellness. Although Freud's ideas were heavily influenced by thermodynamic theories of energy (energy release), he did introduce the notion of personal history, i.e., that understanding requires an historical perspective. Piaget greatly expanded on the importance of personal history in childhood development. Darwin's theories on natural selection as the mechanism of evolution, and Mendel's work on genes – the "how" of the mechanism – were widely discussed. Neo-Darwinism, the genes plus natural selection, is still a debated subject in biology, particularly at the detail level. However, Gullivan's interest in this branch of science was in the distinction between evolutionary change and developmental change (what is the future going to look like in general and in the particular), and the understanding of the limitations in each of the two classes of change.

After World War II, the above ideas became more pervasive, as the old order, the "British Empire," began to break down; of great significance was invention of the transistor, the fruits of quantum physics, Shannon's work on transmitting messages over electric wires with arbitrarily low error, the age of nuclear physics, the great expansion of everyday chemistry, with its multiplicity of new materials and products, the belief in science, the future is science, on to the moon. In 1956, Rachel Carson wrote *Silent Spring*, a book that changed our worldview. We became aware, more aware of our relationship to our environment, our inter-dependence. It is interesting to note that it took seven years to develop the language, the practical process, and then to pass our first environmental piece of legislation. The 60's saw many of the above ideas come into action; the civil rights legislation, the rise of feminism and an increasing number of women making a living outside the home. In the 70's, the idea that "father knows best" had lost its legitimacy. Objectivity, authority of "central," was dead. To put it in the words of Heinz von Foerster, *objectivity*, the properties of the observer, shall not enter into the description of "his" observations (reality is given by fact and we are detached from it). *Post objectivity*, the description of observations, shall reveal the properties of the observer (observer cannot be separated from the situation being observed, and in fact, co-constructs the situation).

For a few more months, Gullivan read through the piles of economic statistics, studies on energy, trade, and felt at times that the whole problem about the next 20 years was just too complex. Although he was indeed frustrated, the sound of "hypothetic deductive methodology" rang in his mind; there must be some simple organizing principles. He remembers this period well, as to when he first understood that prior to solving complex problems, there is a necessary period of unease and that the solution comes not by analysis by deduction or even by ordinary languaging. It comes intuitively. You just see it clearly. By this time Gullivan realized that the Zen Master had presented him with a koan, a type of problem that cannot be solved by "thinking," but only by insight.

About that time one afternoon Gullivan was cutting the grass in the field behind his 200-year-old Pennsylvania farmhouse when he suddenly "saw" the complexity give away. He rushed inside and sat down and wrote as fast as he could, the pencil moving for over four hours. There were indeed some simple principles by which he could let the "data" organize itself. Some of these organizing principles were as follows:

1. Economic growth is a reflection of man's need for security, and taken to extreme, results in ordinary greed.

2. In all social systems (people, businesses, nations), people always act in their self-interest, which is historically rooted.

3. Experientially, through trial and error, people adapt to natural stress caused by changes, in the interplay of technical, economic and sociopolitical factors. They adapt according to their history.

He then played out the historical economic data against these principles. At this point, in mid-1980, his mind was reasonably clear about what was going on and what was likely to unfold over the next several decades,

Gullivan wrote out a draft of how he saw the future unfolding. Then a new problem arose. How does he explain this "picture" to anyone else, particularly the Cardinals? Thus began the difficult and seemingly never-ending process of "defending his thesis." A discussion at one level resulted in many questions which, when resolved, gave rise to additional questions at a higher level. Many times he was accused of jumping to conclusions without having the data to back them up. He became aware that the listeners had not gone through the "process," hence were disturbed by some of his projections. He also believed that it was, indeed, common to assume that the speaker could not "know" inasmuch as the listeners did not know. It took significant periods of time for people to accept his premises and be persuaded of his conclusions. He felt that understanding could only come from seeing a self-consistent whole that operated against a set of principles, rather than trying to explain independent behaviors of the pieces. For example, trying to forecast world trade dynamics without considering the dynamics of technology and the realities of national self-interest and history was futile.

The ultimate presentation to the conclave was "put together by committee." It was difficult to deliver since it was not his natural flow, and he had been advised not to bring up certain embarrassing points, such as the mature state of one of the then admired "growth" businesses. After he had completed the presentation, he looked around the room. He had the strange recognition that the sixteen Cardinals and Courtesans there all looked very much alike. The sixteen looked at one another and then looked to the most senior among them for a suitable reaction to what they had just heard. One of them gave a little chuckle, which triggered the same reaction from several others. The tension was broken, a relief flooded into the room. The first chuckler asked, "How does this help me run my business tomorrow?" More chuckles and more relief. Gullivan felt that his approach to a difficult and important subject had been dismissed, that serious and most probably painful discussions as to what to do about his predictions had been avoided, and quietly everyone in the room had agreed without having to say a word. This event Gullivan remembers very well, as an example of how unpleasant news or topics are dealt with at the court. If the news can be ridiculed to some extent, then the court can allay its own anxieties and uncertainty as to what to do. However, Gullivan had learned an important lesson – let the artist detach himself from his art.

During the following year, the presentation was given to over 100 audiences, both inside and outside Macromol. Some of the ideas and language persist today, some 20-plus years later. The key points in the presentation (then called Context 2000 or just "the context"), supported with substantial quantitative detail, economic forecasts and explanations, and delivered in a set of 35-mm color slides, were:

1. They were entering a period of disinflation and oil prices were going to fall.

2. The world was going to "solidify" into four sociopolitical and economic zones, the Americas, Euro-Africa, Russia, and Sino-Japan.

3. World trade would expand faster than world GNP (leading to what we call today globalization).

4. The late 80's would see an outbreak of peace; the Russian path was not sustainable and would fall apart.

5. Capital investment in synthetic strings was rapidly moving to "noncompetitive."

6. The center of gravity for string production was moving to China.

7. We were about to begin the up-phase of a Kondratieff wave, with significant technological change and capitalist expansion.

After finishing this context, Gullivan concluded that the "future," at least for about 20 years out, is more, rather than less, predictable on a macro scale. The business of predicting the future is a very difficult job, emotional and intellectual, requiring a process of deep immersion, confusion and persistence, from which the scenario emerges as described above. However, even after mapping out a highly reasonable future following such a rationale, it is not necessarily discussable, even at the highest levels. It tends to be drowned out by the concerns of the day and the reluctance to spend the energy necessary to get comfortable with the complexities of the map. As Gullivan will note later, this is to be expected and is not necessarily a problem. There are perhaps better ways to deal with strategic issues in a "future" context, or indeed, with strategic thinking itself.

In addition to looking at global trends and regional economies, Gullivan was also examining the "economy" at a business level, for the businesses that existed in Macromol. These more detailed studies led him to ask a different though related class of questions, the most central of which was, "What is wealth and how is it created?" He had developed a fairly good understanding of the U.S. economy and to a lesser extent, the world economy. And he was well acquainted with the worldwide market dynamics, pricing and cost history, and projections of Macromol's businesses.

During that time (1981) a decision was made to raise string prices in real terms. Gullivan's macro analysis predicted that string demand would fall as a result. This prediction was not politically acceptable, so the chief of Macromol's planning section asked Gullivan to explain how he had come to that conclusion. Gullivan explained that the macro approach took into account final expenditures in the general economy, distribution of profitability along industry value chains, historical productivity levels by industry, maturity of technologies, and their ability to affect future productivity improvement, and finally the ability to accept and pass through price changes within the value chains. The macro analysis was presented on a "spatial diagram," which he told the chief planner was a fairly accurate, though not precise picture. A bottom-up analysis could give you a precisely inaccurate picture. Despite his explanation, the chief planner commissioned a 6-to-9 month classical bottom-up analysis ($500 million in today's dollars) on the expected effect of price change on demand. The well-paid team doing the "inductive" study did not like the idea that one could deduce the answer from macro-economic data, and was quite shocked to learn that their extensive study confirmed the macro deduction. The results were well hidden to protect a more optimistic demand forecast. From this point, Gullivan began to trust the top-down approach, i.e., market or economy back, as opposed to the analytical view from the inside out. The latter approach, he felt, was subject to strategic errors caused by unconscious biases or wishful thinking, or indeed, political pressure. Although a tougher and more mysterious process, he felt it was better to deduce the answer through a top-down thinking approach, rather than derive it from an analysis of historical data.

As Gullivan looked back, the late 70's was a time or pessimism, the days of the misery index, stagflation, and rising oil prices, and he had visited MIT on many occasions to discuss economics and oil price forecasts. A frequent topic of discussion was the apparent decline in total factor productivity in the U.S. economy from 2-3% per year in the 50's and 60's, to 0.5-1% per year in the 70's. Projecting from this sorry state, most forecasts were for economic growth of 2-2.5% per year for the 80's. There was a similarly gloomy forecast for oil prices, ranging from $60-$600/bbl (oil barrel) by the mid-to-late 80's. Gullivan's own view, based on energy use, finding rate, productivity and political factors, was that oil prices were going to fall significantly. This view, which he presented several times, was not "politically correct" and, indeed, he was told sometime later that the espousal of this view was not "career enhancing."

While working on Context 2000, he read much of the classic work on economic development. He was particularly impressed by Nordhaus's work on productivity, which introduced him to capital productivity and total factor productivity (capital, labor, and energy all interactively combined). Several Technical/ Counters, who were competent in both micro- and macro-economic matters, had done some very insightful work on price/ volume distribution by market analysis of competitive behavior in one to many competitors, and the growth equation of how new products propagate. Although much of this work was somewhat arcane and did not find a ready audience, it was of great interest to Gullivan.

Nordhaus, in his work on productivity, broke the economy down by sector, e.g., food, clothing, transportation, etc., and analyzed sector productivity by input of capital, energy and labor. Gullivan's interest in this work arose from the gloomy debate about future productivity in the U.S. and the vision that the 50's and 60's were not typical, reflecting the special circumstances of the massive rebuilding effort following World War II. With the help of others Gullivan was able to examine historical performance metrics of the businesses in Macromol (pricing, volume, margins, investments, etc.). Gullivan plotted the data many ways to gain some productivity dynamics. One member of his group, who knew the mat business very well, had forecast a 2% growth in square yards of carpet per year, based on housing starts and the change in living space in general. Using the macro approach, Gullivan developed an explanation for the rapid growth of carpet that occurred in the 60's by looking at the relationship between real price declines and the demand for mats. He also showed the symmetrical behavior between price changes in cotton, polyester and acrylics. The interdependence of these prices was another unpopular viewpoint. The chiefs were about to make major investments in string for mats, even in the face of rising prices. It didn't make sense to Gullivan. The macro constraints did not appear to fit with the local enthusiasm.

Gullivan traveled to a house of economists to assist with their computer models to break down all personal consumption expenditures in the economy into natural and self-consistent sub-economies using repetitive statistical techniques to "reveal" their dynamics, much like Nordhaus had done earlier. This was a very educational exercise, since the economists were not used to looking at the economy in this way and did not consider food "money" any different from leisure or medical "money." Eventually, having accounted for all expenditures in 26 groups, and then, using statistical techniques, Gullivan and the economists reduced those to 13 sectors without much loss in meaning. This macro view of economic dynamics became the logical place to start. There was clear evidence that one did not use "food money," or that share of personal consumption dollars dedicated to food, for buying mats. Household expenditures could be subdivided into segments such as furniture, cleaning products, etc., so by the process of elimination one could develop reasonable constraints on the total money available for mats. These constraints from the "top-down" approach, combined with the "bottom-up" detailed string price/volume data, gave a realistic picture of how the mat market segment really worked. Gullivan drew the following operating principles from this analysis:

1. At the aggregate (or biological) level, there are no new markets.

2. Technology changes the manner in which basic needs are met, within each sector, and sometimes across multiple sectors.

3. The state of development of a country is reflected in the share of personal consumption expenditures going to food, clothing and shelter. The greater the percentage going to meet these basic human needs, the less is available for purchases in other sectors.

4. The value of a new product can be determined by the top-down approach, by understanding the cost of meeting the need with existing products.

5. When a sector's share of total consumption goes down, e.g. food from 40% just after WWII to around 20% today, the sector is not under stress. When the sector's share rises, e.g. medical costs from 9% in the early 80's to >15% today, the stress generated will produce significant social and technological change. In these cases, resist the temptation to extrapolate the trend. Also, pay attention to the rate of change in these sectors. If it is increasing though decelerating, increasing product sales into the sector may not materialize as expected.

At this point Gullivan had much data and analysis and some insights, and was firmly convinced of the value of using top-down macro-economic analysis to reveal the constraints or boundary conditions with which development and/ or investment could take place and earn an acceptable return. Given the picture he had constructed, the justification for major investment in string for mats seemed quite dubious; demand and price forecasts into the 80's seemed much too optimistic. As Gullivan said earlier, reviews of this work were not well received or understood. He was convinced there must be some way to arrive at some simple rules and constraints that would make better sense of the mountains of data. Analysis begets analysis, and indeed, provides a good living for many, but you don't lose weight by weighing yourself, as he was fond of saying at the time. He remembered his earlier studies on thermodynamics. The laws of thermodynamics are constraints. They delineate what is possible and what is not possible, e.g., how much energy or work one can extract from burning a lump of coal. Surely there must be some level of isomorphism between energy and work efficiency on one hand, and money, production and investment on the other.

What makes a good investment and how to recognize it as such?

All function is an effect of structure.

As Einstein (1936) said, "The world of science is nothing more than a refinement of everyday thinking. It is for this reason that the critical thinking of the physicist cannot possibly be restricted to the examination of concepts in his own specific field. He cannot proceed without considering critically a much more difficult problem, the problem of analyzing the nature of everyday thinking." Science has a long history, going back to the ancient Egyptians and Greeks. The scientist tries to discover the "laws of nature." Some would call this the search for truth. Gullivan felt he preferred to see it as the search for useful explanations, particularly around what is possible and what is destined to happen. In Newton's time, people knew if you first threw a small stone as hard as you could and then threw a large stone as hard as you could, the small stone would accelerate faster as it left your hand. Newton gave this everyday observation rigorous mathematical form in the law of gravitation which has been called the "greatest generalization achieved by the human mind." "Gravity is an explanation," in the words of Gregory Bateson, and as we all know, an extremely useful explanation. It was just such a general explanation that Gullivan was after.

The science of thermodynamics deals with heat, energy and work flows. At first it was thought that heat was conserved, i.e., it was neither lost nor gained in total. However, Joule showed that this was not so. Lord Kelvin was bothered by this and the discomfort led him to discover that energy, not heat, is conserved, which formed the basis for the first law of thermodynamics. The second law is about more constraints and has a long history. Carnot, associated with the French military, posed a problem for himself. Why do the British ships have more power (based on steam) than the French ships? He was determined to find out how to make more efficient, powerful engines. In the process, he discovered the laws governing the maximum amount of work that could be extracted from a given amount of heat in a steam engine, or conversely, the intrinsic inefficiency of the conversion of heat to work. By solving a series of puzzles, other insights followed. One was, that although energy is conserved, the distribution of energy changes in an irreversible manner – a system tends to "cool down," not the reverse. It is this observable and irreversible process of change that gives us the sense of time. What is energy? This is still the great mystery, but suffice it to say that energy's usefulness is its capacity to do work. This capacity is measurable, and the manipulation of this capacity formed the foundation for the Industrial Revolution, converting heat into work in its myriad of forms. During the Industrial Revolution, gains in wealth were driven by improving social productivity by reducing the cost of a unit of work with increasingly complex machines. Machines augmented the muscles just as horses did, so it is not surprising that machines are rated in units of horsepower. The second law explains how much work we can extract from a given quantity of heat. It also informs us that not all of the heat can be converted to work. Something is always lost in the process.

At this point, Gullivan thought that it might be useful to look at some definitions, or perhaps the nature of the definitions. Heat and work are methods, not things. Heat is the name of a method for transferring energy; so also is work. When we consider hot and cold, we use temperature. Temperature is a difference, the difference from the reference point of absolute zero. Absolute zero is the temperature where all atomic motion ceases; it is a temperature not achievable in principle (the Third Law). The name given to the loss incurred in converting heat to work is entropy. Entropy is a measure of the quality of energy. For example, a bucket of coal is a higher quality of energy than ground up coal spread all over the yard. When I burn the coal to heat a room, the energy contained in the relatively small volume of coal is now dispersed throughout the room, or up the chimney. There is no less energy in the room and up the chimney, having burned the coal, but it is now of lower quality; its entropy has increased. The process cannot be reversed, it proceeds in one direction only; you cannot burn a lump of coal twice. Entropy always increases when we warm ourselves, or when we do work of any kind. All of these ideas can be expressed in elegant mathematical expressions, which are extremely practical and are used in a wide range of disciplines. In Gullivan's case, it gave him a framework for thinking about the power of an idea or concept to organize, that is, to increase order locally (economic gain), while increasing disorder in the larger environment through heat loss and other forms of waste.

Toward the end of the 19th century, Ludwig Boltzmann developed an understanding of thermodynamics at the atomic level, connecting our observations at a human scale (the macro-state) with processes beyond our normal perception (the micro-state). The approach that Boltzmann took, deducing a theory to fit the facts, had an important impact on Einstein. As noted earlier, the prevailing approach in science was to derive theory inductively, i.e., to build it up from the observable data. What appealed to Einstein was that the laws of thermodynamics, as expressed in statistical thermodynamics, could be wielded as restrictive principles with no dependency on assumptions about the constitution of matter itself. This is, in essence, the idea behind systems theory, which was to emerge a half-century later, a subject Gullivan returns to later. Einstein adopted this top-down, or deductive approach (i.e., inference from principle), and in 1936 wrote, "There is no inductive method (inference from observation/data) which could lead to the fundamental concepts of physics. Failure to understand this fact constituted the basic philosophical error of so many investigators of the 19th century."

Gullivan began to try to map the ideas of the restricting or limiting principles of thermodynamics onto economic theory. After all, thermodynamics has much in common with everyday economics. We apply work to relatively unorganized material (sand, oil, undeveloped land) to transform materials to create products which are more ordered and have, as a result, greater utility or value. For example, iron ore is smelted to pig iron and ultimately converted to steel when carbon (from charcoal) is combined with the iron ore in the presence of oxygen and much heat. From the relatively disordered state of ore and wood to the ordered state of steel necessitates the application of tremendous amounts of energy and work. How well we organize the transformation influences the degree of economic gain which is extracted. To do the work we create structure, both mechanical structure (transformation engines or machines) and social "structure" (including know-how, language, rules, procedures, and relationships). That is, part of the energy flowing through the transformation system is directed toward creating new order in the machines and in the social structure. Many economists have recognized the striking similarities between the science of thermodynamics and economics, both of which deal with transformation and irreversibility. Both sciences have their origin in Newtonian mechanics. Of fundamental importance in mechanics is the notion of equilibrium, expressed as bodies tending toward a state of rest. Equilibrium is an ideal, a very useful one despite the fact that it does not exist in actuality, just as absolute zero does not exist, yet it, too, provides a very useful reference point for temperature measurement. Though thermodynamics has moved to the arena of "non-equilibrium" and far from equilibrium, it seemed to Gullivan that economics has not moved very far in this direction and is still cast as if the economy seeks a steady state, and is, indeed, a branch of mathematics, rather than biology.

Perhaps the mapping of economics into thermodynamics may not be possible using an inductive approach, that is, from the level of everyday observation, description and measurement. After all, the self-interest, the history, and the purpose of the economist are quite different from that of the thermodynamicist. They ask different questions and make different distinctions in language. Hence, it is not surprising that much effort to reconcile the two sciences of time has met with great difficulty. The inductive approach demands defining counterparts to energy, entropy, work, heat and temperature in the language of economics. While both systems deal with transformation "engines," and both deal with work (coherent energy), there is no obvious way to find a counterpart to price, value and capital transactions in thermodynamics. How do we account for the concept of enjoyment so fundamental in our lives? After reading a great deal about these difficulties, Gullivan was still convinced there was a one to one correspondence between the two sciences. He decided to take the deductive approach, hoping to discover useful restrictive guidelines which can help distinguish between a good and not-so-good investment and make sense of the everyday data and experience.

In addition to economics and thermodynamics, a third science deals with transformation and irreversibility, the science of biology. In the days of "mechanics," the intellectually fashionable way of thinking about everything in the 18th and 19th centuries, Darwin discovered the "mechanism" of evolution – natural selection. Natural selection is an idea at least as awesome as Newton's idea of gravity. Everyday observations and ideas about evolution have a very long history. It was a much-discussed topic in biological circles for most of the 19th century. Darwin, however, explained how it happened. When Mendel's work on genetics was rediscovered, Neo-Darwinism came into being. Neo-Darwinism is a synthesis of the ideas of natural selection and the underlying explanations provided by the science of genetics. Genetics was unknown to Darwin. Although Gullivan was not formally a biologist, he took great interest in the subject and read most of the well-known books from Darwin to those of modern times, i.e., Neo-Darwinism. The most useful ideas to Gullivan were the nature of its restrictive laws, its irreversibility, the role of chance, the difference between change at the evolutionary level, phylogeny, and at the individual level, ontogeny, or developmental biology. He began to appreciate that there was more than one type of change, which Gullivan expands on later.

Neo-Darwinism said to Gullivan that life evolved on the planet over a very long time through a series of heritable "mistakes," that is, mistakes in the reproduction of the genetic code that could be passed on to the next generation. The expressed mistakes that turned out to be useful at a particular time and place were "selected in." They suited the new situation. That is, they survived, were accumulated and passed on. Within a population, those individuals exhibiting the right "mistakes" that enabled them to better fit their ecosystem, reproduced faster. The favorable variation within the population gained dominance simply because the less favorable variations were eliminated in the process. Success or usefulness of a variation is determined by its *role* in the organism's struggle to make a living – to survive. Evolution proceeds through selecting out the vast majority of "mistakes" which do not better equip an organism to survive and reproduce in an environment at a particular time. Therefore, Neo-Darwinism, enlightened by modern genetics, is really about natural elimination. If the environment changes, the organism, with its previously successful biological strategy for making a living, could be selected out as just not good enough. Natural selection works to eliminate previously successful strategies – a position Gullivan will return to later when he discusses the social side (what is observed in social organizations) of thermodynamics/biology. The other branch of biology, developmental biology, offers many insights on how businesses are born and how they develop. Evolutionary biology gives insights into how they are eliminated.

Thermodynamics, biology and economics are really languages that explain, each in their own way, the process of creating order out of disorder. The people making a living in each of these disciplines have their own viewpoints, languages, and a desire to protect their own intellectual area, but Gullivan has no doubt that the disciplines will continue to converge. To Gullivan, the process of living, working, creating value and taking enjoyment from it all can be expressed in terms of order and disorder. In all three domains of irreversible systems, going from disorder to order involves energy, focused energy, which is the definition of work. This was the starting point from which Gullivan deduced the rest of the explanations around what constitutes a good investment. To begin, Gullivan turned back the clock to the time when a business is born and discovered the restrictive "laws" that governed the process. From that point, he examined that business' development first in economic language, and then in its social dimensions and description. The hope was to be able to generalize useful limitations/explanations that apply broadly to any organization.

Again, in summary, referring back to Einstein's comments on the limitation of inductive thinking and adding the historical perspective, the three sciences or languages of irreversible processes (time's arrow) can be deduced from the concept of order and disorder, and each has evolved to meet the particular needs of the particular investigators; indeed, each has evolved its own language. Thus conversations among biologists, economists and thermodynamicists are rare indeed!

Economic Potential

You can't burn a lump of coal twice.

It was now the beginning of the 80's and, as noted, Gullivan was convinced the answer to his puzzle – how does one recognize, select and amplify a good investment? – lay in the language of thermodynamics, economics and biology. Again, these languages are just different ways of describing the same events depending on the perspective, interest and history of the observer. What interested Gullivan were those constraints that arose in the process of making a living, the process of personal development, the derivation of personal self-interest and personal history. That aspect of making a living, taking some relatively disordered input and transforming it to increase order, could be explained using the language of thermodynamics.

Thermodynamic constructs could also apply to that class of activities where making a living involves reducing uncertainty, a way of creating order or certainty, out of disorder or uncertainty. Many people such as doctors, bankers, analysts, managers, investors, etc. earn a living by reducing uncertainty as opposed to ordering things. At this point Gullivan develops an answer to his question on recognizing and selecting a good investment in the world of physical stuff or things. Later on, he comes back to the domain of certainty and uncertainty as he discusses the fundamental change in the mode of productivity as one goes from the industrial age to the age of abundant resources to facilitate computation and communication.

At that time in the early 80's, Gullivan had developed a fairly detailed understanding of many of the businesses in Macromol and was convinced that he could not find the kind of answers he was looking for in common business language. He was equally convinced that somehow, the language of thermodynamics contained and was the source of satisfactory explanations. He puzzled about what it was he was looking for; he was indeed looking for explanations that would satisfy him and at least satisfy some other people. So, what is an explanation? At this point he remembered what he had read in Gregory Bateson's book, *Mind and Nature*. In his book, Bateson discusses the nature of explanation. He discusses how descriptions and

27

explanations are linked by tautology. We map descriptions onto a tautology to give us an explanation. Tautologies are a class of statement like if A is B, then B is A, or less obviously, the geometry of Euclid or mathematics in general. We find that if we agree that if such and such is true, then we believe it must necessarily follow that so and so is true; that is, that validity arises at a junction of the internal statements that connect the propositions. Gullivan was indeed looking for a tautology – a statement that would seem obvious, a foundation statement onto which one could map a description – a description of the business to get a useful explanation. Gullivan thought that it is obvious that it takes work to tidy, or order, an untidy or disordered room. From that one can determine how much one might be willing to pay someone else to do the job. Gullivan's explanations will get somewhat more complex but can, in principle, be reduced to the above example.

After much searching and reflection, Gullivan decided to select a simple example as a starting point from which to build toward a satisfactory explanation. He selected a very familiar though discrete step: that of going from a polymer soup (a precursor) to a fully formed string just as one goes from concrete to concrete blocks. In between the polymer and the string were a transformation engine and a social system (a spinning machine and a group of knowledgeable workers). At this point Gullivan focused on the transformation engine and its potential efficiency and discusses the interrelated social system later.

Looking at engines and what thermodynamics tells us about how to explain their potential efficiency, one finds that an engine's efficiency depends on (along with other factors such as design, friction, etc.) the difference between the "hot" source, say the gasoline burning temperature and the "cold sink," the cooling system. The power of the engine depends on the rate the energy (gasoline) passes through the system. So Gullivan was interested in the hot source, the cold source and the rate of energy passing through. However, since he was interested in increasing order or value, he turned to an example of a machine system which increased order, namely a refrigerator. We take in, he said, relatively warm water of little value, and cool it, thus increasing the internal order to give us a more valuable product, namely ice. So he concluded that all stuff-related activity could be mapped onto a model of a refrigerator. Now strictly speaking the efficiency (potential) of a refrigerator is determined by the difference in temperature between the hot sink and the cold sink, divided by the temperature of the cold sink (or disorder - order divided by order); however, he decided to interchange order and disorder to make the equation yield a whole number and make it intuitively more accessible. It is written as:

(Order – Disorder) divided by Disorder

This reality translates into economic terms, giving us the following equation:

$$\text{Economic Potential} = \frac{\text{Value of output (order)} - \text{Lowest cost of input (disorder)}}{\text{Lowest cost of input (disorder)}}$$

Now this little equation looks a bit obvious. Everyone knows that if you get some readily available material and work on it to create a high value output you can make a fortune. At this level of observation, just the difference, not a lot can be explained. However, the simple concept of economic potential as stated, which "closes" the system by recognizing the disordered input is acted upon or worked upon (the difference divided by the disordered input), can explain a great deal. Economic potential is not as simple as it looks and many people who stated or implied that they understood it showed, by their questions and actions, that they did not really grasp its significance. Its significance lies in the capacity to arrive at a satisfactory answer to the question, "Should I invest, use power or work, in this system?" It leads one to ask the *critical* questions, "What is the value of the output (ordered state) and what is the lower limit of the cost of the input (the disordered state) in question, and what must happen in order to reach this limit, or in some cases, now that I have approached this limit point, what is the wisdom of investing further in this system?" Its importance or explanatory power lies in the questions it raises.

To see how this tautology maps onto descriptions to give explanations, let's look at some examples, taking the case of a set of polymers which were converted to string through transformation machines. Let's ask the question, "What was the economic potential of the particular system before the transformation work even started?" To do that, Gullivan needed to know the value of the output and the lowest possible cost of the input.

Taking the question of value, we first assume, as noted earlier, that man (biologically speaking) does not change in any substantial way over time. What changes is, through technology and the accompanying social change, the manner in which he meets his basic needs. For example, we spend 1 hour 22 minutes a day on average moving about (there are only 24 hours in a day). What changes with technology is not the 1 hour 22 minutes, but the distance we can travel in this time. Likewise, Man has always had a need to communicate: technology changed the amount that could be communicated from word of mouth, through smoke signals, to telegraph, to telephone, to multimedia on global scale. The limits (availability) of time and biological energy or bio-cost do not change. What changes through technology and social structure is what can be accomplished within these resource limits, what we call, in general, "productivity." This leads to the conclusion that, at the aggregate level of man's needs – food, clothing, shelter, communication, transportation, health, leisure, etc. – there are no new markets, just better ways to meet basic needs. The better ways to meet needs replace and often eliminate the old ways. Based on these assumptions the "market" always indicates or tells us the value of a new way of meeting functional needs. So assessing economic potential involves determining the functional value of the output. The functional value of the output product or solution includes all costs incurred by the buyer in the transaction – not only the price but all acquisition costs of stress, time, attention, namely the total bio-cost incurred before and then expected after the transaction. This latter factor, buyers' non-price costs, was not so important in the industrial age or in the industrial age business model. However, these costs are of paramount importance in the computational/communication age, or in the new business model, precisely because much can be done with non-physical or "price" factors, and indeed, how replacing physical factors becomes one of the principle targets of productivity and pricing potential.

Price and value are not the same thing. Value deals with all costs to the buyer and deals with the question of what is the game, is the game worth playing? Pricing deals with the question related to how to play the game. In estimating economic potential, it is important to be accurate, that is reflect reality; whereas precision, the degree to which it reflects reality, is less important, that is, the way of thinking is more important than numerical precision.

In Gullivan's particular analysis with a set of strings, he just used historical selling prices as a proxy for value, and at that time the industrial business model was dominant. Later on, Gullivan will have more to say about how the decreasing cost of computation/communication made the industrial business model obsolete and will describe the fundamental differences between these significantly different ways of viewing the business world.

Having established the output for the set of strings, the next task was to establish the lowest input cost of the related polymers. To digress and reflect on the significance of this class of question, let's look at an historical example. In 1968 Carver Mead, the renowned physicist at Cal Tech, asked the power question, "What are the technical limits of very large integrated circuits, based on the known physics (laws) of the day?" This question was the mother of Silicon Valley. From this question, the answer, in the form of Moore's Law, evolved. Moore's Law states that computer chips are halving in price or doubling in power every 18 months. Moore and Andy Grove of Intel Corporation were, of course, in conversation with Carver Mead. The limits question, although simple in form, requires a sophisticated technical understanding to even ask the appropriate questions. Thus, calculating the cost limit is not a trivial exercise; it usually requires a good understanding of the technical factors determining cost, and in addition, a particular way of thinking about these costs that is not how to "do it," but what in principle (technical) can be done. Gullivan will have more to say about the limits question later when we go through an example of strategic thinking.

For his example, Gullivan estimated the lowest cost by calculating the cost based on a *very* large-scale output to minimize the cost of both fixed capital and working capital. Since the input to the input polymer was oil, naturally the price of oil influences the cost of the polymer. However, since the historical data Gullivan used included relatively low cost and stable oil prices, he ignored this factor. Obviously after the 70's, one had to include the oil factor to assess the sensitivity of economic potential to oil prices.

He now had the output value and the lowest input cost. He then plotted the economic potential over time for four different strings; strong string, comfort string, elastic string and super-strong string. Now the economic potential is a pure positive number; strong string, in its initial life back in the mid- to early-30's, was at least 16. By 1972, the economic potential had reached almost 1. The difference between the value of 16 and 1 reflects the original ignorance in the system or the potential productivity gain for someone who chooses to invest to take the ignorance out of the system, to achieve this productivity gain which is inherent in the system. At a value of 16, we can recognize a good investment at least for someone. Again, Gullivan recalls the dismal outlook by economists in the 70's when many of them were puzzled by the drop in productivity – total factor productivity (which includes capital as well as labor and energy) – from the 2-3% range in the 50's and 60's to the 1-0.5% range (annually) in the 70's and 80's, which led them to underestimate future growth. He concluded that there was no mystery there; one just has to take the time and effort to figure out the economic potential of the main factors or activities determining productivity at the time. In the 50's and 60's there were many activities like strong string in the U.S. economy. It was the late stages of the industrial age, the age of chemistry and new materials in general, which contained high productivity potential, e.g., the whole array of synthetic materials, air conditioning, new fuels, new machines, etc. By the 70's these economic potentials had run their course. Whereas investment, particularly R&D investment was highly productive in the 50's and 60's in their activities, this was not so in the 70's and 80's and on. It was not until the late 80's-90's that productivity in the U.S. economic began to rise to the 2-3% range, the fruits of the computational/communication age, where low cost computation/communication became the principle mode of productivity. Again, Gullivan discusses this later when he describes the fundamental differences between the industrial age (in which low-cost energy was the underlying driver) and the new economy business models (in which low-cost computation and communication becomes the new driver with the impact of reducing uncertainty in all transactions).

To return to strong string, when the economic potential number gets close to 1, the system is well understood by many players, the original well of ignorance is exhausted and productivity potential is very limited. Hence beyond this point, real prices can no longer fall since one can only expect volume to increase at the population level or the GNP level unless, of course, one is considering taking market share from another competitor in the "exhausted" business. Although the business can no longer look forward to significant productivity gains (which is manifest in high margins), this does not necessarily indicate that one should exit the business. If one has a good competitive position or is close to "monopoly," the business can be an excellent cash generator, a resource to finance new lines of R&D. You might think that this is obvious, and normal business practice is to invest R&D resources in new inherent productive activities as soon as the economic potential of the old business is exhausted. However, this seldom happens. The mystery of why so many bad investments are made is the topic Gullivan discusses in the latter part of this book.

Next consider comfort string. It started in the 50's at an economic potential of about 18, but its life cycle was much shorter. By the late 60's it had reached full maturity. This difference in the rate of productivity potential exhaustion between strong string and comfort string reflects competitive pressures. It reflects the total R&D of all companies or even universities engaged in removing ignorance in the system, the discovery process, and not just the R&D within a single company. It is important, therefore, in assessing economic potential, and assessing investment potential, to include all resources working in the relevant discovery process to take ignorance out of the system.

The next string, elastic string, is an interesting case as, although it started a little later than the others at 17, it has had a relatively slow decline representing the slower overall rate of development or transmission of the technology in general, thus leading to company specific know how, low competitive pressure, and the resulting maintenance of high margins (selling price - cost, i.e. surplus). When I refer to the rate of development, I am referring to the total rate for all relevant activities in the total world economy. If a local group is the only group spending resources in the development or discovery process, they can, and do in effect, modulate the rate of decline in the economic potential. This elastic string represents a good business; however, it is susceptible to rapid change, significant price pressure if there is a significant change in amount or distribution of development or discovery resources. The competitive landscape can change almost "overnight"; it is less stable, less predictable than strong string or comfort string.

The economic potential of super-strong string started off fairly low, about 5. It was a great technical success, but the cost of the input was very high. Correspondingly, the market opportunity was limited by the prices required to attain a satisfactory rate of return. Super strong string had reached its mature state by the early 80's, a point Gullivan was not supposed to discuss at his meeting with the Courtesans or Cardinals or at the Context 2000 presentation which was discussed earlier. Since the market determines demand as a function of price, in the case of super-strong string, the focus might well have been on the high input cost, which again is a highly technical matter. However, it was difficult to get this class of conversation going in the early 80's in Macromol.

At this point, one might say that there are no surprising findings here. After all, Gullivan did map a set of descriptions onto a tautology. However, there are some very important conceptual factors to note. The economic potential way of thinking allows for a convergence, a narrower and narrower focus on the question, "Is this a good investment?" It can start with just an organizing principle, an idea, some new way of organizing the disorganized, and does not require much "financial" input data, it does not require precision. All that is needed is a rough idea of the value of the "new solution" and a "technical" basis for estimating how low the input cost can go. Again, the economic potential way of thinking allows one to converge on what must happen in order to reach the cost limit, one can delineate and order in which manner the ignorance must be removed to reach the limit, i.e., one starts from the theoretical limit and works backwards – back-planning. With back-planning, the task of R&D, resource allocation, becomes much less of a gamble, less an exercise in wishful thinking. It becomes deductible, deliberate and accountable. It is in essence a deterministic system, although that reality is often hard to sell.

This approach is essentially the opposite to the usual practice of starting from where you are, looking forward with the usual return on investment analysis. The usual approach of starting from where you are tends to ignore the role of local history, the history is silent, and the process itself is divergent. It contains no mechanism for detecting and correcting fundamental error. In summary, the economic potential way of thinking, the top-down approach, the deductive process, the whole systems approach put the limitations in the business space, its history and prospect in clear view. So the first question to ask in the puzzle of how to recognize, select and amplify a good investment is, "What is the economic potential?"

At this point, Gullivan felt he had the first half of the problem puzzle solved, i.e., he had a good explanatory theory. He could recognize and begin to define an investment with possibility – define to the extent that he could make good decisions on what was worth finding out. More specifically, to design what transformation engine he should invest in; to decide on a plan to find out what he needed to know to increase the efficiency of the transformation engine; and to plan the R&D to find answers to specific questions in a predetermined order so as to search the inherent limits of the system to achieve its full economic potential. In short, to wisely allocate resources to drive uncertainty out of the system and gain confidence in the wisdom of investing in this arena.

Gullivan made a presentation of his ideas to the Cardinal in charge of new business strategies in Macromol. After the presentation, the Cardinal, who was not altogether comfortable with rigorous thinking, remarked, "It can't be that simple!" Gullivan thought to himself, perhaps the Cardinal did not want to see that it might just be that simple, inasmuch as the Cardinal might feel that he really wasn't needed or that important. Gullivan was aware of the level of effort required to develop a sound understanding of the principles involved, the effort to go through the deductive process itself to arrive at the clarity of understanding as to what investments are appropriate. This part Gullivan called writing the play, a difficult undertaking. The second part Gullivan referred to as the performance, which in itself requires the talent to get one's message across. On his journey, Gullivan noted that these two parts were often confused, mixed together, leading to inaction or sometimes unwise action. How often had he heard the admonition – they won't go for that, you have to tell them what they want to hear! At this point, Gullivan asked himself, why is this so? After all, this is the Age of Reason; we are all acting rationally, looking out for the best interests of Macromol. Gullivan wondered if this assumption of reason was an illusion (or just an idea in good currency), so he decided to look at the social and economic evolution of Macromol over the past few decades.

Economic Potential and Social Norms

No question is so difficult to answer as that to which the answer is obvious.
– George Bernard Shaw

The cost of belonging is the path not taken.

After learning another lesson – the Cardinal's need to be seen to be needed is important – Gullivan's thoughts turned to reflecting on the conversation, the ideas, the rules of the game and social behavior in general during the development of the economic potential, the discovery and making of the various strings in Macromol. Gullivan decided to start in the 50's and describe how it was in Macromol, to describe the social climate decade by decade up to the early 80's and map it onto the economic potential curve. To each decade he assigned a color to reflect his sense of "hotness," or state of emotional and intellectual intensity to best characterize the period. He also selected those prevailing ideas, or conversations that seemed in "good currency," or what the prevailing truth was in each decade. What statements the Prince pronounced, that in turn influenced the course of events, the "choice" of behavior in Macromol. The 50's he characterized as the "Red Phase," the 60's as the "Orange Phase," the 70's as the "Green Phase" and the 80's as the "Blue

Phase." The 90's were, for Gullivan, the time in which those in Macromol could continue on their path or strike out in new "Red" directions as they had done in the past. Would it get deep Blue or go Blue/Red?

The Red Phase

The 50's, the Red Phase, was the time of high technological drama. The scouts from Macromol ventured out into Not Macromol to hire the best and the brightest, especially with respect to the Technicals. A community of Technicals, both scientists and engineers, was formed. This community was the best in all of Macromol and Not Macromol, with respect to all aspects of discovering and making string; strong string, comfortable string; elastic string, and later, super-strong string. Consequently, Macromol had the lowest cost of string making, all the necessary resources were there, and the tribes worked very closely together. The goals were clearly stated in technical, production, economic language. The relationship between clarity and validity (economic potential) or purpose, resource utilization and competence gave rise to the glory days at Macromol. New products emerged in a continuous stream, profit margins were high and it seemed that there was no end to the valid problems to be solved, to the future business opportunities. There was what Gullivan called a climate of expanding ego space. The ego space, the space for personal development, career development, and career advancement seemed unbounded. The climate in the Red Phase was decidedly "intellectual." The path to successful career advancement to the level of Courtier or Cardinal was biased toward technical prowess. In this technical climate, vigorous debate over technical matters, the best path to pursue, was common place, even at the level of the Cardinals. Personal passion in debate was not out of place. At that time, it was the norm to attend technical conferences, deliver papers, and to continue to attract the best and the brightest. The intellectual climate demanded a very high degree of preparation to rigorously "defend" a recommended course of action, inasmuch as many of the Cardinals were both technically literate and rigorous. Indeed, the prevailing rules of promotion often emphasized intellectual and technical ability over so-called leadership qualities. The Red Phase was also a time of expanding technical distinctions, definitions, discoveries, and indeed a time of expanding language.

The Orange Phase

The 60's, the Orange Phase time, was in many ways a continuation of the Red Phase, but with increasing emphasis on production economics. It was in many cases the time of the second production facility for a given kind of string. New products such as elastic string and later, super-strong string, began to take off. Engineering was now on a par with science. The Orange times also reflected the desire to expand overseas, to expand the geographical boundaries of Macromol. A special unit was formed to find out the best ways to use the various products abroad in Europe and Asia, thus expanding the market space and influence of Macromol. Although many continued to go to technical meetings and conferences, production and production management theories became increasingly important. The new product programs continued to be clearly targeted, the goals were clear, progress was easily measured against clear goals. Measurement technologies such as PERT and management by objectives became increasingly popular. The career path continued to be biased toward technical prowess, but now also included broad experience in different modes of production, and different production facilities. In technical and broader business discussions and meetings, a rigorous and disciplined approach was still expected. In new product development, teams of Technicals, Makers, Persuaders and Counters formed naturally, and against clear goals, progress and contribution were easily measured. As in the Red Phase, the ego space, the space of possibilities seemed boundless; there was a sense of optimism and security. With the surplus of resources, new product domains were explored. One significant new product, non-tearable paper made from special string, was discovered and developed. This development was interesting in that it took a lot of time, and indeed, a failure to recover the original investment to get this product beyond the take-off point and into the profitable zone. Other attempts at new product domains used up considerable resources, but never made it into the profitable zone. Something was happening to the capacity to create a surplus out of a surplus in those "adjacent" new product domains.

Perhaps the economic potential was running down or, indeed, out. Reflecting back on the Orange Phase, the technical conversations and discussions were beginning to settle down. They had less novelty, less surprise. The technical and production short-hand acronyms appeared more frequently. Macromol had created its own language, a narrower and more specific language in which the time to reach agreement to give instructions narrowed. Thus, as efficiency in production increased, so did the efficiency of language or conversation increase? Conversations deemed off "the point" were excluded, the consequences of which Gullivan returns to later. Although the language narrowed, optimism still prevailed. On one occasion, during a visit by a Technical Cardinal to discuss Gullivan's own activities and programs, he revealed that he just wanted to know how Gullivan was developing his successor.

The Green Phase

The 70's, the Green Phase, was a time of major transition, both inside Macromol and outside in Not Macromol. With ever increasing success in making, production, and production efficiency, the focus shifted from creating and producing, to producing and selling (or persuading). Indeed, the inhabitants of Macromol could produce more than they could sell. Macromol continued to expand its influence and operations internationally. A major change in abundance, the cost of the primary inputs, namely oil and natural gas in the early 70's, altered the economic, potential, and thus, the profitability of string making businesses. Apart from the rise in the cost of the inputs, perhaps more importantly, many in Not Macromol had learned how to make similar string products. Macromol no longer had a privileged position in many kinds of string making. Thus, the ignorance that characterized the string making activities in the early Red Phase was no longer so, the major problems had been solved and that knowledge was widely distributed, thus, intense competition led to the lower selling prices, lower margins, lower overall surplus. The glory days, the time of optimism was fading. Questions were raised by the Prince as to the wisdom of devoting so many resources, so much surplus, to technical activities, to the promise of discovery, especially since it had been sometime by then that a major new product success had "come out of the laboratory."

This was also the political time in the Not Macromol world when the negative side effects of string making activities received increasing attention.

Rachel Carson's book, *Silent Spring*, was working its way through the political consciousness, and environmental regulations were gaining in acceptance. The 70's saw a remarkable change in the "truth" and how the "truth" was constructed. In line with the realities of exhausted, or matured, Economic Potential and the political climate of environmentalism, the balance of power (the truth) began to shift from the Technicals, to the Makers, to the Dealers. In 1975, Macromol had a negative surplus, and in the eminent MIT professor Don Schön's words, we were moving beyond the (dynamically) stable state (*Beyond the Stable State*). In a sort of coup d'état, the Technicals lost power in the summer of 1978. This event, of course, changed the rules of the game, and people had to adjust their activities, their truth, their method of achieving what they wanted, i.e., their strategies to meet the new realty. It was noteworthy the Technical high priests, the Fellows, were now less valued than their administrative counterparts. During the Green Phase, people went to a plethora of courses – writing courses, listening courses, and personal development courses – to develop skills that the new management field now considered appropriate. Perhaps for social reasons these courses were popular in that they kept people, and managers, busy and gave the illusion of purposeful and productive activity, or "skill" development. Meanwhile, business meetings became less focused, less targeted, less disciplined and, to Gullivan at least, more "social" and more confusing. Following the work by the club of Rome, technology planning, scenario planning and similar ideas came into "good currency."

The age of anxiety had arrived, and with it some very important changes in the rules of promotion. Price pressures, cost pressures changed the climate to where the ability to cut costs, analyze the data, were more prized than intellectual or technical ability. More importantly, however, at least in Gullivan's view, was the change to a "go along, get along" climate, the faith in the idea that the Prince and the Cardinals "knew" where they were going and that the rest should follow. These factors assumed increasing importance in promotion decisions. Don't rock the boat! It was clear that the spate of possibilities, the ego space was closing, thus personal energy was increasingly focused inward, dissipated in the anxiety rather than in the useful coherent action. As Plato remarked, "What is honored is produced." Out of the preaching of the management gurus came a particular disease, the birth of the idea of human resources. With this bad idea came two managers, one to run the program and one to run something else. Gullivan still did not know, except for such obvious and necessary activities such as abiding by and having clear policies related to the many laws on "working conditions" what real contribution they made. Thus, responsibility for personal development, and accountability for results became diffuse, which Gullivan thought was a big step backwards. In the Not Macromol world, a very powerful set of ideas was beginning to grow, the ideas and beliefs in the philosophy of Hayek (1964 Nobel Laureate in economics), namely deregulation or laissez-faire economics. These ideas were about to have a major transformational impact on the Anglo-Saxon economies, and indeed, the lives of those in Macromol.

The Blue Phase

The Blue Phase, the 80's, began in a general climate of high oil/gas prices, stagflation, the misery index, anxiety and relative insecurity. This anxiety about the future, and the imaginary doubt about Macromol's access to vital inputs, oil/gas, led the Prince to buy, for a high price, an island that spoke the language of, and engaged in, the activities of oil/gas. On the other side to security questions the Prince, an unusually technically competent Prince, led Macromol into a new domain, the domain of life sciences, or biological chemistry. With this decision came new investments, the hiring of a new class of Technicals. With this entry into a new space of possibilities, Macromol was "poised" to enter a new Red Phase, perhaps. In the early Blue Phase of the 80's, there were two opposing forces, the forces of dynamic conservatism, the forces that focused on the activities of the day, on reducing costs, the methods and politics of counters, and the forces striving to create new spaces of opportunity, and on the need to innovate. The Blue period represented the to and fro of the struggle for the truth between these opposing forces, these different versions as to what was important, what resources one should devote to conservatism or creation.

Meanwhile, consistent with the ideas of Anglo-Saxon philosophers, deregulation, personal development, the management gurus began a massive outpouring of advice. Thus, a whole new class of conversations became politically important in Macromol. The cost-cutting Cardinals, attuned to the demands of the deregulating market, brought about the first major, and somewhat voluntary, reduction in the population of Macromol. The voluntary program, which exceeded expectations, indeed, led to the significant reduction in cost. However, though seen by the market as a positive move, a move to greater efficiency, it was none other than the transferring of assets, human assets, to the current earnings column. This was to give the illusion of increased surplus, rather than in reality the sale of social assets and the devolution of Macromol, an illusion that persisted for another two decades. The Cardinals could not in their conversations find employment – productive employment – for those who left Macromol. In that exodus many of the inhabitants took with them the memory of the Red Phase, and the discipline required to give rise to, and to grow a red star. The business meeting was changing, changing significantly, in that the rigor and discipline of the past was no longer reasonable. The drive to short term surpluses, presumably driven by market concerns, gave rise in many instances to a climate of wishful thinking, overly optimistic sales forecasts, and in some cases overly optimistic future prices. In many ways it reflected the business school language, the language of disembodied rationalism, the language of those detached from the power, the self-interest, and the daily activities of those making a living in the business. The multiple forms of analysis, ways of describing capital costs, ways of describing surplus, etc. became fashionable. This fascination with the numbers was augmented with the availability of computers. The analyses grew longer, the charts more elaborate, and the whole conversation became more and more removed from the people in the activities of the business itself. It seemed as if everything was measured over and over again as if you could lose weight by weighing yourself. Soon the goals were set about in imaginary numbers, detached numbers, and not grounded in specific business activities. Strategies become numerical fantasies, not methods to get what you wanted.

The Prince began over again to question the resources devoted to research and development. He noted the poor return on the multibillion-dollar investment in R&D over the period 1975 to 1985. Many people supplied answers to justify the continuation of the practice, but as far as Gullivan knew, nobody asked the key question: what was the economic potential, the state of non-ignorance in the areas of investigation or research; was it possible in principle to have created a "good return?" A thoughtful analysis of the latter would have shown that the poor return was, indeed, predictable though the story was not politically popular.

Almost as if to fill the vacuum left by exhausted economic potential, the new management fads became increasingly popular and indeed politically correct. Technical literacy, technical questions, intellectual rigor, one might say even serious questions, were frowned upon. This was the time of the emergence of what Gullivan likes to call mythical leadership. Instead of business of management meetings, they now had leadership meetings, which, of course, make the distinction between the in-leadership and the out-followership.

There was the belief that business success lay in climbing up obstacle courses, swinging off ropes, leading each other around blindfolded, all to build a sense of feeling good about the future. There were sensitivity courses, sexual harassment courses, ethics courses, so many courses that Gullivan can't remember them all. Valuing people became the mantra as those still in Macromol headed into their second "early retirement" program. The buzz-words, the aesthetics of the charts, became more important than real content, yes, the medium became message. One of the interesting buzzwords was "intra-preneuring," which sounds good but in a Blue Phase is internally inconsistent. There was no space for radical ideas, nor can there be in the climate of mythic leadership. One had to give birth to adults, adult businesses, not start at the beginning with the baby. This, indeed, was the time of denial, as one can readily see by reading the annual reports from Macromol, or the internal conversations related to strategic direction. There was a curve for the declining businesses, a curve for "stable" businesses, and a curve for future businesses. Nowhere was there a description of what had to be done to get there. Inasmuch as a strategy is a method of getting what you want, there was no strategy, no mechanism. The forces of creation were, however, still active in the Blue Phase.

By the mid-80's, there were at least a couple of dozen people, mostly the Technicals in Macromol, who had a good grasp of the major technological and scientific developments underway and likely to form the basis for future discovery and development in Not Macromol. They understood the potential of these new domains and their technologies' relevance to Macromol. Assuming the concept of the "rational man," as Gullivan did then, it appeared to him that they were trying to recreate the past, and could not step out into the future. What was going on? They had many very bright people, Cardinals and Courtiers, all busy trying to make a living. They had ample financial resources. In the social area, Macromol was probably unsurpassed in its ethical stance, in its fair and equitable treatment of the inhabitants, i.e., it was remarkably well endowed. It occurred to Gullivan that there was something else going on, or perhaps different explanatory systems were necessary to make sense out of what was happening, perhaps explanatory systems that focused on the non-rational domain. They seemed to be in some sort of survival mode where just holding onto one's job, making it through to retirement, were the primary concerns. The survival anxiety and sense of insecurity, instability made it difficult to call on the emotional energy required to take on new challenges. Gullivan decided to develop a better understanding of the sociopolitical factors in general, and how those factors were playing out in Macromol around 1985.

Gullivan recalled what he had learned in business school many years earlier. One of the courses he took was on market failures. In science and in medicine, one learns through failures, not successes. The vast majority of the then-current business school books or consultants emphasized, lauded, told and retold about the successes. In Gullivan's experience that data approach taken by the vast majority of these authors led to conclusions that were at least ten years behind what people in business already knew and, indeed, were already doing. Nowhere, however, in these books is the language history of the particular companies taken into account, at least in a manner that reflects the constraints on the then-current options. Nowhere was the reality of daily business, making a living, the concern of the individual over his or her own job security, job or career prospects, promotion, getting along with colleagues, the nature of truth and power taken into account. Gullivan could not recall a serious discussion of the real politics within the corporation, the struggle for power, the questions of who talks to whom and about what, how is the internal "truth" constructed and how is it conserved. It seemed a bit like going to a doctor who studied anatomy, but had no real experience with live patients, so does not have an ongoing relationship with a particular patient. Gullivan found these books to be not very useful, and in many respects quite harmful. He felt that they were and are harmful in that they are fads, such as the latest on "chaos" or "biology" or "democracy" or value chain analysis.

The wise reject what they think, not what they see. – Huang-Po

Amidst all the internal noise in Macromol and the recession across the land, Gullivan decided to travel to the centers of technology to learn of potentially new organizing principles. He felt it was time to re-examine technology in general, as much had happened since the earlier work on the Context 2000 presentation. He laid out a plan of action and "hit the road." With his colleague, Richard, Gullivan visited a wide range of universities, MIT, Harvard, Brown, Cal Tech, UC Santa Barbara, etc. They also read a great deal of technical literature. Of particular interest was the work done by OTA (Congressional Office of Technology Assessment) and published in a 1988 report, "Technology and the American Economic Transition – Choices for the Future." When their fact-finding mission was over, Gullivan and Richard structured what they had learned into a simple chart. The chart, now many years old, still reflects future technological possibilities. At the center was a box containing three words – chemistry, computation and communication. Around this core were three main areas of technological development – information technology, biotechnology, and new materials. Even though they had a good understanding of these areas, they could not write out a set of organizing principles which would guide investment action. Thus began for Gullivan a fairly intensive quest to discover the simple rules governing the use of these technologies.

He started with information technology, since it seemed to him that that was the fundamental technology, the one that informed the others, that indeed made the other technologies, biotechnology and new materials, possible. The process of understanding information technology was that of immersion, once again. He read a great deal. He was very much influenced by Pierce's book on information theory, Gregory Bateson's book on communication, and the work of the second-order cyberneticists, the science of control in controlling systems, George Glider's many books, and Jeremy Campbell's *Grammatical Man*. He went to many conferences, spanning a wide range of informational technology perspectives. There were two tracts to the search for simplicity, one technical, the hardware, and the other software and the social system. He finally collapsed it down to a set of statements, which as organizing principles reflected its potential productivity: "the reduction in the cost of communication and computation facilitates the reduction of uncertainty in economic activity." The mode of productivity is in replacing excess "stuff" which is now used to handle uncertainty with information. The nervous system organizes itself to compute a stable state, and since communication and computational technology are extensions of the nervous system, value or productivity arises in the context of individual uncertainty reduction, and expansion of the space of possibilities. These factors determine the design of a potentially productive business model. Gullivan discusses a particular case later on and how the above statements guide the process.

The second area, biotechnology, was equally challenging. Again he read a great deal, much of which was from "Scientific American" and a wide range of technical publications available at the time. The book that Gullivan found most useful and most strategic was *Signs of Life*, by Robert Pollack. He mapped biotechnology/biology onto language which in turn led one to see biotechnology as information-based chemistry, where the molecules "read" each other as in Braille, i.e., read by touch. This biology/biotechnology is about harnessing this "Braille" based chemistry to produce appropriate molecules. In contrast, traditional chemistry is based on "bubble, bubble, toil and trouble," i.e., cook the ingredients under controlled conditions of temperature (and perhaps catalysts), clean up the mess to get the pure product, and then perhaps shape its form. The efficiency potential of chemistry is fairly well understood in the domains of thermodynamics, reaction, kinetics, catalysts, chemical engineering, etc., and is well suited to the mass production of relatively simple molecules. This is particularly so if oil/gas remains fairly abundant. So the near term (20 years) productivity potential of biotechnology lies in using the Braille based chemistry to make complex molecules or to alter or redesign living systems to alter the kind or rate of output of desired molecules or materials.

Biotechnology or Braille based chemistry may well be the preferred route to complex molecules, but what again about relatively simple molecules? Gullivan started to delve into this question, i.e. which of the two chemistries was best suited now, and perhaps over the next 20 years, to produce relatively simple molecules. This question could be resolved using consideration of (1) the relative abundance, i.e., lowest cost at a given level of complexity of the input and (2) the comparative thermodynamic efficiency of classical chemistry and the Krebs cycle in Braille chemistry. He had begun to do this work when discussion of biotechnology at Macromol seemed to fly in all directions, so Gullivan changed his focus to a promising area in new materials.

The New Materials

A superior vessel takes a long time to complete. – Zen Proverb

In the midst of all this noise, Gullivan got an opportunity to put his ideas on economic potential to direct use. In the early 80's there was much activity in the string department focused on new business opportunities. One of the potential opportunities was identified as composites. Composite materials are made from strong, stiff strings such as carbon strings, glass strings or Kevlar® strings. These strings are held together with suitable polymer materials such as "epoxies," the choice of polymer depending on the conditions the composites material had to withstand in terms of heat, pressure, corrosion, etc. The technical people in Macromol were very familiar with these materials, their chemistry and their use. The emerging market or business opportunity seemed natural and appropriate to us at Macromol. Gullivan sat through many planning meetings, where market opportunities and other factors were discussed, but always left with the feeling that we really didn't have a good understanding of the subject – there was little clarity. The center of gravity of these activities moved from the strings department to central research and development department, and Gullivan, being outside of this social system, lost track of what was going on for a while.

One day Peter, a friend of Gullivan, called to inform him that he had been appointed planning manager for composites, an example of the new materials. He felt that Gullivan was familiar with the difficulties of developing a strategic plan so he asked him to help. Gullivan began an intense involvement with strategic thinking in composite materials. Although there were many people involved and many studies underway, Gullivan wanted to focus on some of the central ideas in the strategic thinking process. His question was "why composites?" What is so special or remarkable about these materials? He knew that he did not really understand these materials. So he asked himself, who in the world knew most about composite materials? When he discovered that this person was Professor Gordon of Reading University in England, he invited him to spend a few days with them in Macromol. Gullivan was very impressed with Professor Gordon's understanding of, not only composite materials, but of materials and structures in general. In his remarkable book, *Structures, or Why Things Don't Fall Down,* he relates engineering principles and materials properties to everyday problems. It became clear to Gullivan that the road to understanding composite structures was to start with fundamental engineering principles, from the top down to the specifics. So, why composites, from this perspective?

The fundamental reason for composite structures is that one can line up the strings in the right direction corresponding to the expected load. That is, one can design for isotropic or unidirectional force lines as opposed to metals or ceramics where the force lines went in all directions. Secondly, composite materials were much lighter than metals. They could achieve the engineering requirements at a much lower overall weight than metals such as aluminum, titanium, steel, etc. Thirdly, through choice of plastic polymer matrix material, that is the polymer that holds the strings in place, one could design for a range of conditions of pressure, temperature, corrosion, etc. There was a fourth factor of great future significance. One could relatively easily imbed microchips in the polymer string matrix. Thus, one could see this technology evolving into intelligent material systems, where the whole structure could sense and respond to conditions of load, e.g., the wings of aircraft could flex to adjust to flying conditions, or a submarine could respond to and cancel out sonar signals from another vessel.

To Gullivan these organizing principles dominated the potentials for these relatively new materials. They could organize all the data they had or could raise the right questions to ask, to determine what they needed to know. To do this Gullivan teamed up with Dick, a real expert in economic evaluations, manipulations and organization of a lot of data. Dick and Gullivan started with an overview of all the relevant materials used in the economy and noted the importance of special properties such as weight per unit strength or stiffness, resistance to harsh environments, etc. The opportunities for composite structures depended on successful "engineering" of these structures so that they could substitute for "metals" at specific price points. They arrived at a measure of value of composite structures as a function of price. The next question, "What was the lowest potential cost for these composite materials?" This work involved a considerable amount of detailed analysis of chemical and engineering factors as related to the various strings and matrix polymers, and the composite manufacturing process of putting the composite together. In meetings with some of their Technical colleagues, where they tried to discuss the results of their analysis of the lowest potential cost of carbon string based on the known physics, they met with much resistance.

These rather strange and unusual meetings brought home to Gullivan for the first time the difficulties that arise when a complex subject is viewed from an atypical point of view, from a different point of ignorance. Our individual domains of ignorance stem from our history, the questions we have asked and the answers we have found. These domains of ignorance are in what we don't know. The area of ignorance of the scientist, with his knowledge of what is known in his field, is quite different from the non-scientist, who in most cases does not even know what bothers the scientist. The Technical group viewed the problem in the usual way, how do they get from here, from what we know, to the lowest potential cost, which Dick and Gullivan had described, and had given the reasons and assumption for their position. Their position was based on the physics, the theoretical amount of energy required to form the carbon strings, i.e., the theoretically lowest cost. Since the Technical group did not know how to think about achieving the lowest possible cost, they got frustrated, claimed the cost position was unrealistic, after all the Japanese were working on this for several years and they say this is the lowest cost they can achieve. Why should we in Macromol be able to do any better? But, as discussed above, the proper question was not how can we do better than the Japanese, but rather how can we manifest the economic potential in the carbon string system?

What surprised Gullivan was the difficulty encountered in getting the Technical group to let go of the desire to solve the problem and to get them to focus on what the problem was – the technical issues that have to be solved in principle to get to the lowest cost position? What is it that they knew that they did not know? This latter class of mental activity is very difficult, frustrating and, even if possible or "allowed," it is avoided. It is more satisfying to demonstrate ability in one's area of expertise, to "solve" one's particular view of the problem, than it is to question the technical validity of the problem in the first place. This is in a sense a version of the bias for action and a need to display one's special ability: let's stop discussing theory and get on with it; we have done the strategic planning, now let's implement. This politically correct way of dismissing the burdensome task of critical thinking is at the heart of the problem in strategic thinking or planning, i.e., making the distinction between a sound and an unsound investment.

Lao-tzu said about 2500 years ago, "There are no fixed judgments of right and wrong in the world. People each judge as right whatever they consider pleasant, and judge as wrong whatever they consider unpleasant." The senior Technical people, the Fellows, were all comfortable with discussion about their areas of expertise. After all, they were promoted and honored for that expertise. Their histories reflected a narrowing of their area of interest – they had become specialists. Is it surprising that they became ill at ease when the topic shifted to "What is it you know you don't know? Let us now openly discuss our ignorance."

Dick and Gullivan continued to deepen their understanding of the "lowest potential cost," for various inputs such as, for example, carbon string. It was clear to them that one of the key technical factors in decreasing carbon string costs was heat management. Carbon strings were made by essentially burning off or carbonizing acrylic strings. The huge hot ovens were very expensive and essentially heated the neighborhood. The solution lay in "local heat control," a problem solvable in principle even though they or nobody else knew how to solve this problem (at that time). Gullivan, however, felt that with advancements in electronic control, this was a solvable technical problem, a problem of resources, focus and discovery, not invention and, if solved could result in a huge pay-off. By then, they had a good grasp of functional value, and lowest potential cost, and calculated the economic potential as 14, fairly close to 16, the number strong string had at its beginning. However, the applicable market space was much greater for composite materials than it was for a strong string. As noted above, the process of developing the economic potential provides the answers to the technical questions, "What does 'anyone' need to know, to find out, in order to go down the economic potential curve, what is the nature of the ignorance in the system from 'end point' to now, i.e., backwards in time?"

There was another class of questions which related to non-technical factors, e.g., market access, history of relevant competences, financial factors, competitive factors, etc., which they also needed to answer. With all of the relevant and required abilities (disciplines) for anyone to succeed accounted for, they were then ready to play the competitive game. They analyzed each potential player according to their strength in the required disciplines. They noted where each competitor was weak or did not have specific disciplines. They rated the individual disciplines by the relative criticality to "winning" the game. Particular attention was paid to when a competitor lacked entry to market, or was critically weak in a particular discipline. They then estimated the cost, the investment that any planner would have to make in order to have a chance of winning, to be fully adapted to winning. They had 10 possible players, so now they could estimate what it would cost all players to equip themselves fully to win. Obviously the player with the lowest total cost is the player with the best current position and is favored to win. They could now specify what investment, in dollars and competence, Macromol needed to make to be in a winning position.

With the strategic analysis done, how does one convince the investors to invest? As you may note throughout this book, the next problem arises from the previous problem. Both problem, and indeed, purpose, always arise from the background or context. However, the background or context is bounded; its boundaries arise from the history of the organization or social system. The language and what is discussable is bounded, and has hidden limitations. Consultants from Not Macromol were hired to look at a range of potential business opportunities, so Gullivan and Dick took advantage of the presence of the outsiders. They structured the presentation that outside consultants made to the Cardinals. This process was quite successful. They also developed a rigorous political "planning" process where specific members of their team were assigned the task of teaching the key Courtesans and Cardinals all about the language of composite structures and its relationship to Macromol's self-interest. The initial multi-million-dollar investment was approved by the Cardinals. The search was then on for the right person to lead the new venture. A new chief was appointed. A four-day planning meeting was held to scope out future action. Dick and Gullivan went through the strategic analysis and explained how they could specify market opportunity by market and by selling price, based on a top-down analysis. The analysis yielded a general view of the volume potential at a given price. The technical factors determining real cost, thus potential real price declines, were discussed, i.e., they outlined the potential "experience curve," the economic potential by general market. The meeting was very intense and Gullivan remembers it well. Most of the participants were not used to the top-down or deductive approach to strategic analysis, and indeed, it was obvious that the chief had doubts as to the feasibility of developing a specific "price/volume distribution curve" for each market. In a few weeks they had a detailed breakdown of the world aviation business by price/volume and what needed to happen. This analysis was key to gaining the necessary additional resources, technical and marketing, to "get into business."

This analysis was followed by similar work on other key markets. The analysis of the "hostile environment market," i.e., chemical reactors, was particularly interesting and instructive. They had much standard market research type of data. The data was gathered from the perspective of a polymer scientist and market researcher, i.e., it was essentially inductive and from an internal and historical point of view. Once again, Gullivan was unhappy with the "data." It did not make much sense to him. There were essentially no general guiding principles to determine its accuracy or its credibility. He puzzled over this during the late summer of 1984. For a while, Gullivan was quite disturbed by his failure to make sense out of the market potential for these new composited materials, and perhaps later, "intelligent" material systems, materials that had sensors and actuators imbedded in them. Then, once more, he recognized that he had acquired another koan. While digging in the garden he suddenly just knew – he should start from fundamental engineering principles and not the data: the lever, the inclined plane, rotational motion, the chemistry, the conditions of pressure, temperature, corrosion, etc. While this may sound obvious, this approach caused considerable friction in several meetings. The next morning he arrived a little late, as he often did, to the meeting with the Market Research group and the rest of the team. Gullivan started talking, making the marketing people unhappy with this intrusion into their presentation (with many charts and lots of data) and, indeed, into their territory. However, the senior Technical man, Joe, who knew Gullivan well and how he thought, said, ok, let's listen to Gullivan.

Gullivan and a few Technicals worked through the difficult process, down from "first principles" and arrived at a set of parameters which constrained the data and provided a very operational set of principles by which they could "recognize" a valid opportunity and indicate what they had to do to get there. The key principles were stamped on a blue mug. This process became known as the blue mug approach, and although Gullivan got a director's award for that work, he felt that few people understood the deductive nature of the process or how atypical it was. After that, the composite structures venture went through a series of personnel changes, the dark shadows of the Blue Phase. Courtesans who were "available" were brought into the venture, few of whom understood the strategic factors. They brought their own history and perspective. The Persuaders took over, and Dick and Gullivan faded from the picture. It seemed to Gullivan in retrospect that the rigor of the deductive approach, the awareness of the underlying "why" of composites, was lost, and language and processes became more and more wishful, short term, and political. The institutional memory of the Red Phase with its emphasis on intellectual rigor, technical ability, potential and the capacity to build had been lost, perhaps many years earlier. A few years later the conversations about composites were aborted.

Gullivan sensed that perhaps the people now in Macromol could not let go of the past, get back on their feet. He felt he had hit the wall and wondered if indeed it was possible to bring about change in a previously very successful community. Once again it was time to visit the outside world. This time, however, it was not about technology but about us: Why do social systems participate in their own decay, make bad investments, and forget how to make generative ones?

BOOK III

IN SEARCH OF TEACHERS AND ENTER THE JESTER[1]

*To speak truth to power is illusionary – it cannot be heard.
If the wrong person preaches a right teaching, even a right teaching
becomes wrong. If the right person expounds a wrong teaching,
even a wrong teaching becomes right. – Mythic Prince*

One morning, while shaving, Gullivan looked into the mirror. There he saw what looked like a Jester. He intuitively knew what that meant. He was now playing the role of the Jester in Macromol. When speaking privately, he spoke and acted as Gullivan, but when he spoke to the court, he played the role of the Jester.

The approach to trying to unravel what was going on in Macromol based on the notion that man is a rational animal has its place in technical matters, but its usefulness in understanding the politics, why people made the decisions they made, the investments they made, what could and could not be discussed was seriously limited. Gullivan had to go on a new journey to find out why very talented people and groups of people seemed to make quick and bad decisions. Gullivan knew it was time to adopt the role of Jester in Macromol at certain times and places. The Jester can speak "truth" to power, but must do so in a manner that is somewhat mysterious, half serious so that which he speaks can be dismissed, can be ridiculed. This stance allows the Cardinals to take cover when needed. However, Gullivan knew that, once spoken, what is said is henceforth never unsaid. He noted in the past, people often declared that they did not understand what he was talking about, only to tell him months or even years later, what he had said, word for word and indeed, what it meant. Additionally, Gullivan remembered Shakespeare. To kill the Jester is

---

1 Book III may be skipped on first reading. Book IV moves to answers while this section contains detailed insights from Gullivan's teachers, including further background on a social system's natural resistances to change and the relationship of power to "truth" and dogma.

indeed a serious misdeed, so the role of Jester provided a measure of political and emotional security.

It was a beautiful day mid-August 1985, when Gullivan got off the plane in Vancouver, on his way to the American Cybernetics Society. At the Airport he met Paul and as they drove down town to the university, Paul told Gullivan that he wanted to introduce him to a very interesting friend of his. Later that evening, in a local pub, Paul introduced Gullivan to Gordon Pask. Gordon, a somewhat short and frail man dressed in dark clothes and a cape, was sitting across from the Jester while his right hand leaned on his umbrella. Yes, indeed, Gordon was very British, the quintessential actor whose demeanor fluctuated between a broad smile and an intense focus. As Gordon and Gullivan began to talk, Gullivan noted and sensed that this man knew something important, important to Gullivan, even though Gullivan could not quite follow what he was talking about. Gordon was talking about conversation theory, now what was that? Gullivan thought, "How could one develop a theory about something as ordinary as every-day conversation?" Gordon proceeded to discuss P-Individuals, M-Individuals, entailment meshes, the torus and a lot of mathematical concepts that went right over Gullivan's head, yet he continued to listen to Gordon. He later began to read the many papers Gordon had given him. Still somewhat intrigued and perplexed, Gullivan left the conference on the fifth and last day with a deep koan. Over the next few weeks, he tried to read several of Gordon's papers again, and then for a while, Gordon and conversation theory faded as other concerns came to the fore.

In early October of that year, while Gullivan was in the process of the final grass cutting in the fall, he almost went straight into the large walnut tree. He stopped the mower. He suddenly sensed an understanding of what Gordon was trying to tell him, and from that time on, he no longer considered conversation as trivial, but as central to our way of living. Gullivan's awareness of himself, his life and his language had fundamentally changed. He thought of conversation as an ongoing search for meaning, of self-identification as a process which goes around and around and every so often there is a sort of collapse of complexity, the birth of meaning. Gordon's entailment meshes reminded Gullivan of quantum mechanics where, as in Schrödinger's Cat, the world or meaning arises when we observe, make a measurement, and collapse the system, as if in a recursive dance we enact our awareness. Gordon seemed to arrive at his worldview from the interface between his experience as an actor and his experience in mathematics, computers and mechanical devices, so it took Gullivan many months to get some sense of clarity in his own mind as to what Gordon was trying to tell him.

Over the course of time in many more conversations with Gordon, Paul and others, Gullivan felt that the following represented the most important insights relevant to his question to understand why human social systems behaved as they do. According to Gordon, every topic, or part of a conversation is derived or produced from other previous topics. Each topic is derived from at least two other topics. This point reminded Gullivan of all "higher" forms of life: life arises through sex (excluding the asexual forms), the exchange of two appropriate sets of chromosomes or "genes," and indeed, Gullivan asked himself if this is also how inventions occur, a subject he will discuss at greater length later on. According to Gordon, the process of conversation is circular, recursive, there are no basic units, and there is no inherent hierarchy. Conversation, either with oneself or with another, is the process of learning and understanding, that state of "collapse of complexity" is personal to the learner. As the person in the conversation discards bits and pieces in the process of conversation, the collapse of complexity, this simplification gives the appearance of sense of a hierarchical structure, a beginning and end. In the process of conversations, one is always listening, simplifying and arriving at what might be regarded as useful structures, and then testing and validating these temporary, seemingly useful structures or bits of meaning-making. Again, it is personal and historically dependent, and for most people leads to internal resolution. A few are able to live with internal discord, which at times then leads them to creation.

Perhaps most disturbing to Gullivan was Gordon's conclusion: yes, there is no music in the piano. There is no such thing (outside language) as knowledge, objective knowledge. There is no knowledge in books. There are knowers. This stance, of course, the purveyors of knowledge management will not want to hear, to know. This is a dangerous idea. Since knowing is personal, Gullivan reflected on the occasions when others would "tell" him he did not know such and such. Gullivan often puzzled on this question. How could someone else claim to know what another did or perhaps could not know? Surely they must have meant that, if I, the other, did not know, how could you, Gullivan, know? As Gordon noted, personal knowledge is not open to inspection, and indeed, that is why we converse, how we come to understand, through repeated recursive conversations to "limit an error" in our mutual assessment of what the other knows. I think I know now what you think, and on and on. Thus, Gullivan began to realize that he was writing his own narrative, his life's story in conversation with himself and others; however, it was not until he met Humberto Maturana and his conversation about the language of biology, or the biology of language rather than the languages of mathematics, machines, computers, physics, etc., that Gullivan felt an embodied sense of language.

Gullivan now asked himself "How does one think about the problem of making bad investments?" As he discussed before, in the mid-80's, the Prince at the time asked the question: "We have invested over $12 billion in R&D over the past decade, so why have we failed to come up with any new blockbuster products or businesses?" Many people in Macromol gave explanations ranging from "look at all the new products that were developed" to "we need to work harder on our R&D." The new products, however, were the result of classification; that is, considering all minor improvements as new products, and did not represent substantial progress. Based on his viewpoint, the question asked was the wrong question. As noted earlier, the question Gullivan asked himself was, "What was the economic potential inherent in the arc of research activity?" His answer to this question was that the poor performance reflected the fact that the area of search, research, was fully mature as reflected by economic potential analysis, so that it was not possible in principle to have gotten any other result. Furthermore, working harder or even smarter in the same context could not, in principle, yield much improvement. The mine was exhausted. When he tried to voice his opinion on numerous occasions, using the language of thermodynamics, "you can't burn a lump of coal twice," he mostly experienced blank stares, silence, and marginalization. He began to realize that he was drifting outside the standard language, the way of seeing that prevailed in Macromol. He was drifting outside the prevailing strategic and historical conversational language. Since he was personally interested in the why of so many bad investments, perhaps in excess of $30 billion since the mid-70's to late-90's, he decided to take the road not taken. He decided that for him it was much more important not to be misunderstood than it was to be understood. This arose from his concern over the common practice of co-option; listening to what he might say and then claim – Oh! We are doing that. His personal puzzlement on why so many bad investments far out-weighed his internal need for social acceptance or popularity. Somewhere along the line, he began to diverge from the ongoing conversations in Macromol, and began to look outside for insight, a way of thinking, a way of explaining, at least to his satisfaction, why so many very large, bad investment decisions. Thus, began his role as the Jester, the Jester who "lived" at court on the island, but whose thoughts and internal conversations moved beyond the conversational confines of Macromol. Gordon Pask had revealed the nature of the Macromol and the non-Macromol conversations and their fundamental differences.

As he had often done in the past, Gullivan read in a somewhat intuitive and random manner, fully aware that the focus, the attention of his concern would show the way. One January in the mid-80's, Gullivan got an invitation to a Gordon Conference in Cybernetics at Oxnard in California. For some intuitive reason, the subject matter appealed to him, so to the conference he went. The first two days at the conference the Jester described as chaotic, confusing and seemed to him to be more driven by issues of radical feminism than anything else. The language, subject matters and discussions, were quite foreign to Gullivan at that time. On the third day, however, Dr. Ulanowicz gave a paper on the thermodynamics of an ecosystem. Dr. Ulanowicz explained in his way how an ecosystem develops, first by increasing mass with little change in information, and then by increasing information (complexity) with little further change in mass. This concept which combined both classes of change he called ascendancy. This concept intrigued Gullivan, and thus began his introduction to the community of second-order cybernetics. First order cybernetics dealt with control and feedback in trivial or machine systems, whereas second-order dealt with the control and feedback in controlling systems, that is, in living systems. By the end of the conference, Gullivan met Frank, an artist, his friend Paul, at least a cybernetician, and Heinz von Foerster, the magician, all of whom, along with many others, became lifelong friends in conversation.

Gullivan cannot remember whether he met Humberto Maturana at that meeting or perhaps a year later, but his thinking was radically changed and most influenced by his conversations with this man. According to Gullivan, Maturana's philosophy, or point of view, or system of explanations, was difficult for many very intelligent people, such as professors in management, social systems, business, gurus to understand. Perhaps this was due to Maturana's care not to be misunderstood or perhaps more likely, according to Gullivan, it was due to the lack of wanting to understand. Most "intellectuals," steeped in the legacy of western and Anglo-Saxon style of thinking, tend to cling to cause and effect explanations, to believe in the notion that the objective world is knowable, and most of all to believe in the objective existence (disembodied) of knowledge: that there is such a reality as instructing the "students." They have, indeed a strong self-interest in the credibility of this point of view inasmuch as many of them make a living in this game. Consequently, why should one want to understand Humberto Maturana? Maturana starts with his own self-selected puzzle – what is perception, what is cognition and what is the nature of a living entity or system? He starts from the history and viewpoint or standpoint of a biologist. His early work as a neurophysiologist was on the question, "what does the frog's eye tell the frog's brain?" We might restate this as, "What does the frog's nervous system tell the frog's eye?" With Maturana's elegant and powerful system of explanation, it is often hard to know just where to start, and indeed, how to proceed. Maturana claims that living and knowing are the same thing and that these concepts are biological phenomenon and they can only be understood in the language of biology. He claims that a living system is essentially a system that makes itself. It is autopoietic, which is, self-making. The components make the components. The living system is a system of interaction; how-ever, these interactions are circular in nature, recursive, and this recursive nature of the interaction is necessary to be alive. The bodies in the morgue are not engaged in internal circular "communication." As Leon Tolstoy noted, simple ideas often lead to great consequences. Such is the case with these simple starting ideas.

Now, if the "communication" of a living system is circular, then that system is organizationally closed. He concludes that all living systems, being closed are, therefore, autonomous. This in turn leads to the conclusion that living systems, themselves, specify how they will interact as a result of any internal or external perturbation. The structure of the system at any given point will determine how the system will behave or interact. If this is so, these closed systems (though thermodynamically open, energy flows through them) do not have input or output instructions. This, then, leads to Maturana's startling conclusion that there is no such "thing" as information. This somewhat disturbing idea does not sit easily with many who have a vested interest in the notion of the objective existence of information, so they understandably dismiss this line of thinking as something they don't want to be "true" or believe, even though with their PC they are aware that the specific internal structure of the PC determines what happens as a result of their "perturbations." If there is no information, then what, for example, is going on in the classroom or say, the business meeting? Yes, we know the answer very well. We know that each person in the business meeting "decided," based on their own history, their own internal structure, what was heard. Each individual will "decide" for himself or herself what they hear, given the same "message." The message is a series of perturbations in the air, 20 beats per second, which perturbs the structure, ear/nervous system of the listener at that moment. What is said is not what is heard. The listener selects. This notion was very evident to me, Gullivan said.

One night on Nightline, Ted Koppel interviewed about a dozen people after the O. J. Simpson trial. Ted introduced each of the participants, relaying to the audience their general background, in essence their belief bias. Each in turn gave the expected answer to a given question. There were no surprises. It is interesting at times to hear the Democrat and Republican views on the "same" political speech. The listener decides, based on the listener's structure, what he or she will select to hear. It is worth remembering that the physicist believed that the "ether," that mysterious substance, carried the light wave along its path. With Einsteinian physics, the "ether" became irrelevant. So, too, with phlogiston, that mysterious substance that left the burning coal. It, too, disappeared into the historical lore. Gullivan wondered where this was all leading, and then said to himself, "What can the investor hear, what are the structural limitations on the strategic conversation?" These questions can now be answered, at least in principle.

Maturana claims that we live in a structure-determined universe. Yes, deterministic, but not Newton's kind of determinism – the clockwork universe of cause and effect, of force, mass and energy. Newton was not a biologist, so naturally he constructed his universe according to his own standpoint. Maturana further claims that if we did not have this structural determinism, the universe would simply be chaotic, unknowable, and hence, we could have no science as we understand it. You could not be reading this book. Gullivan liked to think of it in terms of the pleasure he got from kicking the rugby ball between the goal posts, and what if the structure of the ball were that of maple? He shudders to think of his unwise structural coupling.

Nothing is nowhere, and everything that lives (or indeed is now living) in this structure-determined world is always somewhere. What, indeed, is a horse that is not somewhere? The horse lives in the horse's world. In Maturana's language, the horse is structurally coupled to its environment, to its medium of existence, just as the DNA "lives" in the cell, the unit of life. This point raises the legitimacy of some everyday questions, such as, "Is it nature or nurture?" Can we in fact make a "true" distinction between "nature" and "nurture," except, of course, in everyday conventional language? Is not the unit of relevance the "horse within the horse's world?" Now that we recognize that we are in a structurally deterministic universe, structurally coupled to our environment, inseparable from where we are, and noting the autonomous nature of living systems, we can conclude that the structure of an object or living system determines all of the interaction it will undergo in that "structurally coupled" environment. Maturana is a biologist and unlike Newton, who might be considered to view his physics ahistorically, Maturana sees the world historically. So that structurally determined interaction of the horse with its environment determines its next set of interactions, inasmuch as the "first" interactions alter the structure of the horse. As Gullivan will discuss later in Heinz von Foerster's language, the horse is a structurally deterministic system, state determined, but the horse is not a trivial system like a machine whose input specified its output.

Now, as Gullivan said, if we proceed to look at historically deterministic living, non-trivial systems over the course of history, Maturana takes us to an understanding of language, and a second concept, the conservation of a manner of living, and that which was of most interest to Gullivan, the conservation of a manner of languaging. Maturana proceeds to claim that our everyday notions of cause and effect are not in the domain of biology, but in the domain of language, the domain of descriptions, to ourselves or others, where we are in the domain of the observer, observing either ourselves or other phenomenon. When we operate as observers, we ascribe causality to events, our everyday way of explaining and conversing. We ascribe causal status to an active agent that we say causes (as an observer in the domain of descriptions) such and such to happen. However, Maturana would claim that in the domain of what is operative, the phenomenal domain, it is the structure of the object or the living system that selects the response. So there is no information, there is no "instruction." The system selects its response according to its historical structure. We cannot objectively know the world out there. We can just interact with what is in our environment. Our knowledge of the world out there is always subjective, depending on the history and variety of our interactions with the "out there," and our descriptions as an observer in language of events out there makes distinctions such that it would appear that there was such a reality of cause, effect, control, and in sequences of behavior such a "thing" as hierarchy, instruction, objective existence of knowledge, etc. As Maturana claims, to know is to exist. Intelligence is the structural coupling (successful) that allows a living entity to continue to exist. To exist is to know how to exist. This way of seeing is indeed very familiar to those who live in the East, the Zen master who is aware and lives directly, and recognizes the world of language as illusion, and useful.

Now, Gullivan says, let's proceed to focus on us humans, Homo sapiens sapiens, our more complex structures, say relative to bacteria, are plastic; that is, our structures undergo changes in our ongoing structural coupling with our environment, be that playing tennis or just in conversation. Thus, Maturana claims that this structural plasticity, the ongoing changes of state in our interactions, is learning. We cannot but learn. The question that follows is, "What do we learn?" Well that, of course, depends on the history of our structural coupling. Where have we been and with whom have we conversed? Now, it should be obvious that this learning is both an expanding (new environments) and converging process, converging in the sense that we adopt a worldview, a way of making sense of our world that is satisfactory (historically) to us. As Maturana claims, when the structurally plastic living systems interact, they will automatically evolve, they will co-evolve in a closed pattern of interactions. They will, indeed, form what we might consider a social system. Now this view of a social system, something that evolved historically, is radically different from what the systems theorists, outside the language of biology, talk about. The language of system dynamics is that of a social system where claims are made that the members of the system have purposes of their own and the whole social system has its purpose. The latter stance never gives any insight into the origin of purpose and dubiously ascribes purpose to the "whole" social system in question. Gullivan referred to the many systems people, who in some form or other belong to the "nonbiological" school, people who have written a great deal, have "instructed" a great deal, and indeed, are convinced of the value of their position (how they make a living), but in his experience their input was of little value in finding answers to his questions. Now that Maturana has explained how social systems arise naturally from their structural coupling, they learn as they go, they fit together, their inter-actions become more closely coupled. In the manner of close historical structural coupling, in the case of Homo sapiens sapiens, language naturally arose, the "voice box" and brain size in the language of the evolutionary biologist evolving at the same time. This structural coupling in language, conversations (which is about the coordination of conduct that is recursive) is the medium in which we humans live. So says Gullivan, "I can observe how in Macromol, the structurally plastic learning Homo sapiens sapiens, who are closely coupled, will, over time, develop a 'shared world view' – indeed, their own particular language in which events, observations, expectations and emotions will be explained." The theory of Macromol will necessarily and naturally evolve, converge and the language and interactions of those in Macromol will, to an observer, seem different from other populations. The strategic conversations will be special to Macromol. Conversations held in other islands, for example new technologies, new business models, will not map onto the Macromol language. It will not structurally couple; such conversations will not "want" to be heard. At this point, Gullivan said that he felt comfortable that he had the beginnings of a way of thinking about how bad investment decisions arise naturally in populations that were, from the observer's point of view, previously successful.

Gullivan noted that apart from what was said, there was for him the experience itself during those conversations. He described how, on one occasion, he experienced the feeling or perhaps the emotional response on the part of Cardinal T. Cardinal T. seemed willing to listen, but gave Gullivan the sense that he, the Cardinal, was weighing what was said in terms of how the conversation might play out with the Prince or the other Cardinals. He sensed an emotion of fear and some trepidation on the part of Cardinal T. that those conversations might disturb the current prevailing wisdom, and indeed, might call into question the work done in the recent past, and the Prince's and other Cardinals' comfort level in the adopted strategic conversation, even though he was alone at dinner with Cardinal T. This raised the question for Gullivan: "What really goes on in these conversations, and what is so-called rational thinking, rational action?" Maturana claims that, prior to language, and with non-languaging animals, they coordinated their behavior in structural coupling through their emotioning. The nervous system, including its sensors and actuators, its multiple chemistries of recursive message sending and receiving, selects the response to a perturbation depending on its now state, which of course reflects its history. It lives through emotioning, the structurally determined or automatic body response for that body at that time. With the evolution of language, Homo sapiens sapiens coordinate their interactions, their relations, and their behavior, in what Maturana calls "the consensual braiding of language and emotion" which he calls conversation. When at court, the Jester came to understand conversation in this context, his sense of being, and his sense of awareness changed. He no longer thought of conversations as those long somewhat entertaining diversions from the world of action, but as the very core of being human, albeit a deeper level now than when he began to change through his conversations with Gordon Pask.

For Gullivan, this new awareness deepened the puzzle of where does rationalism fit in. According to Maturana, "Rational behavior began as a feature of the living, of our ancestors with language, in the use that they made of the abstractions of the coherence of their daily living, as they operated as languaging beings." But it was then, as it is now, emotions that specified the domain of rational behavior, in which they operated at any instant. But now we know that every rational domain is founded on basic premises, accepted *a priori*, that is, on emotional grounds – "it feels right" (remember the tautology) – and that it is our emotions that determine the rational domain in which we operate as rational beings at any instant. After a long restful pause, Gullivan recognized as he said, "What is this distinction that G. P. Snow made between the two cultures, the arts and the sciences?" He said that every scientist and artist that he had met was deeply attached, emotionally connected to their theories, their art. Throughout history, distinctions have been made such as the mind/body, objective/subjective and more germane to Gullivan's interest, the distinction between the espoused theory and the theory in action. Such distinctions, though they sound learned, and indeed, have provided the basis for making a living for many, make no sense in the biological explanations of what actually happens. They are language games. Gullivan noted, as Maturana says, "People always do what they want to do," so the Prince in the domain of utterances, performances, espouses what he wants to espouse, what indeed he wants to be heard saying, as we all know from everyday politics. However, the Prince gives speeches and instructions, but acts according to how he wants to act. So much for the distinction. As Maturana says, two things happen in our rational living. One is that we use our reason to support or hide our emotions, and we do so with such frequency that we are not aware of what we do. The other is that usually we are not fully aware of the emotions under which we choose our different rational arguments. The result of this is that we are rarely aware of the fact that it is our emotions that guide our living, even when we claim we are being rational. As Gullivan noted, just reflect on the rational arguments proposed by the Democrats and the Republicans to explain almost anything.

Our failure to understand our living in emotioning gives credence to the rational argument, the man of reason, manipulation through rational behavior. It is, indeed, interesting to reflect on the legitimacy of the celibate priest to instruct his flock, the sheep on how they should sexually behave. But as Gullivan said, the more pertinent question is that of the legitimacy of the business professor, the consultant in many cases, the business guru, who makes a living out of instructing or advising the business person how to run their business. These advisors seldom have the emotional understanding of what actually goes on in the daily life of the business. They seldom have to concern themselves with hiring, firing, meeting a payroll, closing a plant, or sitting all day in a business battle. In the arena of strategic thinking, their starting point is their own "rationality," their own theories of how activities "should" be conducted. They arrive with their laptops, their cluster of eager MBA's, apply their rational logic, rediscover for themselves what is already known, apply the formula and determine how many people lose their jobs. The businessman is often only too happy to pay large sums of money to assuage his own emotional involvement, and point to the rational argument for justification. Gullivan said, however, that he is concerned with the question of how did the condition arise such that the consultants and the intervention were deemed necessary or appropriate. Gullivan said that after many years he concluded that business is best explained as a biological activity, making a living, as all living systems do, and that the rational game is the game of power. Gullivan noted how puzzled he was about the subject of power, rationalism, leadership, and he said that he would discuss these subjects later when he would share the insight he got from Foucault and others. But now, to summarize what he learned from Maturana, Gullivan now felt he was on the right track, the appropriate system of explanations to understand the why of bad investments, and how social systems evolve, and how they "act" now.

Maturana states his first law of systems as "whenever, in a collection of elements, some relations begin to be conserved, a space is opened for everything to change around the relations that are conserved." Maturana notes that we always live in the present, coupled to our environment. We speak now of the past, our history; we speak now of the future, perhaps our hopes. This brings to mind David Ingar's (the Swedish neurophysiologist) point about the concept of future memory. We play out in our minds' scenarios about the future, which we "remember" in the present. We situate ourselves in these scenarios and have an emotional response to the abstraction of us being in that scenario, and perhaps conclude – I don't want to go there. This is how we live. We are structure-determined systems; this is how we make sense of our world. We look to explain things in a structurally determined manner, cause and effect and sometimes to find the guilty party or who is to blame. We always do what we want to do, even though we frequently declare otherwise. Our attachment to rationalism, or what I call disembodied reason, is essentially grounded on basic premises we have accepted *a priori* … our preferences, so rationalism is grounded in our emotions, our history of preferences, and our agreements.

Sometimes we hear people say things or make claims which quite recognizably disturb us, which leads to Maturana's second law of living systems: "The path of living systems in general, and the path of human history in particular, is guided by emotions not resources." A resource becomes so only if you want it. As Maturana points out, we humans live in the medium of language. To understand the enormous power of language, consider the bio-cost a group of non-languaging primates incur versus us. We can tell another where the food is, as opposed to random walk finding.

Based on our particular history, our system of explaining our belief system, we conserve what Maturana calls our manner of living; the Courtier struggles daily to retain his status, his sense of present and future security. In order to do this the individual constantly adapts to circumstances. So the capacity to adapt, or what will be discussed later, the capacity to learn, is also conserved. So Gullivan said, "We need to understand what is conserved in Macromol, what can change, what can be learned."

Gullivan noted that Macromol can be viewed as an ensemble of conversations and agreements. From this point of view, we can see that changes in status of an individual, the creation of new products, the turning on or off of machines, are always preceded by conversation, written or oral. So Gullivan followed the path of conversation, and claimed that the past and future of Macromol depends on who talks to whom and about what, what conversations are possible, and what is the ensemble of conversations that are unlikely or, indeed, not possible. In this context of conversation Gullivan tried to find out what can change, or what can be learned.

Gullivan then asked, "How does one learn?" and remembered that in Maturana's world, learning and living are the same thing. We learn according to our history of where we have been and what we want to do or learn.

Learning and the Nervous System

To live is to learn, but learn what?
Losing an illusion makes you wiser than finding a truth. – Ludwig Börne

Again, Gullivan asked, "What is it to learn and could this subject be further expanded?" He thought, yes, but to do so he needed to understand the work of Ross Ashby, as Maturana suggested he do. Ross Ashby set for himself a very profound question. First he took as his basic assumption that the nervous system behaves adaptively, and secondly that the nervous system is a state-determined system, that it is essentially mechanistic. The fact that it is highly complex, and that, as Heinz von Foerster points out, the "next step" is not computable due to the level of complexity, nonetheless, the nervous system

69

is historical, and deterministic, analytically indeterminable, and hence not predictable. Based on these assumptions, Ashby deduced the necessary and sufficient condition that any mechanism (regardless of material form) must have in order for it to behave adaptively, to change for the better, to learn. His approach was that of rigorous mathematic logic. Gullivan proceeded to narrate (as he saw it) what he found relevant in Ashby's work as described in his book, *Design for a Brain*. Ashby notes that not only do man and other animals learn, change their behavior, but they usually do so for the better, and their survival probabilities increase. Ashby distinguishes between when (a) food is taken in, salivation increases reflex type of behavior that is genetically determined (learned) and not appreciably affected by individual experience, and (b) learned behavior that is not genetically determined but is the result of the organism's individual experiences, or in Maturana's terms its history of structural couplings to its environment. The nervous system which is triggered by incoming stimuli from the senses, must act in such a way that the "nature" (or structure) or each neuron is conditionally relative to each other; i.e. each neuron must have just the right relative "nature" for the whole organism to exhibit relevant behavior. Thus Ashby asks the question, "How can he specify the correct properties for each part if the correctness depends not on the behavior of each part, but on its relations (communication) to other parts? What sort of a machine can be self-coordinating?" In a state determined system this means that each part, if in a particular state internally reflecting a particular state externally, will always behave in one way only.

"When a kitten approaches a fire, its reactions are unpredictable and usually inappropriate; however, the adult cat places itself at just the right distance from the fire, not too hot, not too cold. What has changed, and how did such beneficial change occur?" Ashby then proceeds, "How did the kitten, not yet cat, learn?" He proceeds with his argument, and methodically arrives at the first fundamental point: if an organism affects its environment and the environment affects the organism, such a system is sure to have *feedback*. It is interesting to note that in many animal experiments, and indeed social systems experiments, feedback is eliminated or not allowed, e.g., in Pavlovian experiments, where stimulus evokes a response but the response has no effect on the stimulus, i.e., a one way "conversation," or perhaps one hand clapping. However, in an environment with a simple reflex feedback, an organism, the kitten, may just walk into the fire. What feature keeps it from such potentially fatal action? The living system, the kitten has a set of variables, called "Essential Variables," which are closely linked dynamically and relate to the survival of the kitten, e.g., heart rate, blood pressure, blood oxygen, glucose level, etc. To survive then, the kitten must conserve the value of these variables between the appropriate upper and lower limits. If we take a simple well-known feedback mechanism, say the governor on an engine, we note that as we change the load on the engine, the governor affects the fuel input, thus the system (engine + fuel input + governor) maintains constant engine speed, i.e., it is dynamically stable and the interaction of all the parts dynamically stable. Now, if we consider a live engine system, i.e., a cat, Ashby defines "a form of behavior is adaptive if it maintains the essential variables within physiological limits." If the kitten stays far from the fire, the kitten behavior cannot be called adaptive for temperature – the kitten is cold and not acting homeostatically (in its best interest) for temperature. The cat, on the other hand, sits in just the right position. The cat has learned, adapted, while keeping the essential physiological variables between limits. The cat has a lower bio-cost in maintaining itself "feeling good." The cat's adaptation or learning serves to limit variation of essential variables, just as we do when we build houses, wear appropriate clothing, or even travel by skis rather than walk. We, like other living systems, have through evolution acquired mechanisms to change "learning modules," i.e., behavior according to environmental condition, while keeping the essential variables within limits. Indeed, we may exhibit vigorous change in behavior to maintain "feeling good" or "stable."

At this point Ashby goes from the stable system to what he calls the ultra-stable system. Suppose we consider the kitten's active, or observable part, i.e., the environment, and the internal system (set of possible behaviors) that "acts on" the cat we see. Now the internal system(s) has a distinct set of possible values, so the range of behavior the kitten can exhibit is less than or equal to this set (the law of requisite variety). Now in the simplest most immediate or threatening case, the environment triggers the essential variables (through the nervous system and sensors) and the kitten will exhibit behavior according to one of the possible internal states or possible options. The kitten, in a new or unknown environment, will by trial and error (blind) act to get the essential variable within limits. Thus the kitten or "an organism that can adapt" has a motor output to the environment, and two feedback loops. The first loop (local) consists of its giving the organism no affective information about the world around it (reflexive). The second feedback through the essential variables (including such correlated variables as pain receptors) carries information about whether the essential variables are or are not driven outside the normal limits, and it "tests" the internal states or set of possible options – possible success. The first feedback plays its part *within* each reaction, the second determines which reaction shall take place. Thus, through trial and error, the kitten "finds" the appropriate state (option) that corresponds to the essential variables being within limits, the kitten is "ok." To learn, to find the right or new option (state), *the system must have a second feedback loop* (one for the play of choice and the other for the performance). The new equilibrium will be an adapted one.

Gullivan thought this all rather complex. "What I hear is that stimuli from the environment trigger a check out of the essential variables, those that determine survival, and if one is out of limit, the signal triggers the set of possible strategies or behaviors and selects one which is then enacted by the active or motor part of the organism's system." This acting out now provides new stimuli to the essential variables (the second loop) and through a process of trial and error (in a new environment) the system, the organism reaches equilibrium and that new strategy or behavior at equilibrium becomes the adapted state; indeed, the equilibrium state will always be found to be an adapted one.

Ashby proceeded from that basic double feedback system which meets the necessary and sufficient conditions for a system, a mechanism to change for the better. From that basic premise Ashby proceeds to derive, explain, increasingly complex systems. There are, however, several points that Ashby develops along the way which will become important later. The disturbances in or from the environment can be of two modes, the small frequent disturbances and its feedbacks and the less frequent more significant disturbances which require step changes in the system. As the system finds its way back to equilibrium, these step changes constitute what the biologist calls learning these adaptations, and learnings can be accumulated in complex systems, thus lowering the bio-cost in dealing with similar environments in the future. It is also noted that a large change can be handled if small changes can be made in sequence or independently to accommodate what at first seems a large step change which, of course, reminds us of the process or mechanism of evolution. Large complex systems can form subsystems some of which are highly coordinated and some independent, and indeed, can change from one form to another. This becomes important in complex interaction or tasks that involve many subsystems.

As Ashby illustrated in learning how to drive a car, first learn to control steering, then the accelerator, then the gears, then, if not before, the brakes. As some subsystems in the learner are not involved and others are, the learner will learn to drive cumulatively and progressively. If on the other hand the stimuli from the environment were transmitted down the chain of subsystems, it just might be too much to handle, i.e., too high for the channel capacity. If the stimulus is transmitted bit by bit, overload is avoided. Thus in adapting systems there are occasions when an increase in the amount of communication can be counterproductive. The learning, adapting, is not necessarily confined to communications within the organism. For example, in tennis when the server throws up the ball with his left hand, the position of the ball (in the environment) guides the right arm's action through vision, thus the feedback loop can (and, of course, frequently does) travel from the organism through the environment and back to the organism. As complex systems adapt or learn, they form complex dynamic systems around themselves, e.g., tools, nests, houses, etc. where active defenses make the organism more resistant to changes in the environment.

Environmental disturbance, resulting in disturbance to the essential variables, is also costly. To limit disturbances, every system "simplifies complexity." The entire construct of the "laboratory" provides buffers – we don't see and we don't hear a huge range of complexity in order to deal with simplifications, so that we can learn about the world in parts, sequentially (otherwise we can't do science). Because of our fragile biology, we build "stabilizers" that enable us to more easily maintain the essential variables of biological life, such as houses with roofs and insulation and heating systems. In daily life, habits are simplifications that shield us from too much complexity, only one of the countless examples of cognitive responses to the high bio-cost of living.

Living systems avoid or dismiss complexity – because it is too costly to engage it, and it might even kill them. But to survive as the environment changes, living systems must learn, and learning is costly. A given living system has limits as to the environment to which it can adapt. It may not have the requisite variety (range of suitable behavior options) or capacity to learn fast enough. As observers we can note the significant, natural resistance to learning to adapt to complex environment – the bio-cost is high, and the benefits almost certainly unclear to the beneficiaries. It is possible to amplify learning in an existing system – a child can be taught new words, or can be given a dictionary and "exceed the system's requisite variety" (Ashby). Systems can successfully expand their requisite variety if they learn part-by-part, sequentially; maintain clarity in the local subsystem they are engaged in while learning; and avoid over communication between subsystems.

Now through evolution the learning mechanism was "selected in" for its survival value to the organism. This genetic endowment, the learning mechanism, operates such that part of the learning is left to the environment. For example, the kitten does not learn to catch a mouse from its parents; it is hard-wired to chase small things that move. In other words, the mouse teaches the kitten how to catch a mouse, as we have often noted when the kitten, playing with a trapped mouse, will stay still if the mouse does not move, but immediately moves if the mouse moves. Lastly, learning can be amplified if one subsystem with its variety can, with a small change, trigger a large response in another sub-system(s) with its own limited variety, as noted above when we give the child a dictionary.

So Gullivan said that the "information" or structure that comes via the gene pattern can be augmented by feedback from the environment and thus exceed the limitations of the gene pattern. These ways are the *only ways to learn*. Additionally, an organism with one or many double feedback features will eventually learn, adapt. In other words surviving is learning and what we have learned is a function of genetic endowment and its history of experiences of sequence of environments. In new environments we learn by *trial and error* (the only way). We build resistance to change intentionally through coordinated subsystems (habituation) and externally through active defenses. Such double-loop systems will inevitably tend to adapt to their particular environments, or die trying. So how do we move from these basic abstractions or idealizations to social systems, and how do we and the social group learn?

Gullivan said that we learn and adapt all the time, we learn in the context of the social system. Now some people say the only competitive advantage is the capacity to learn faster than the competition. This may be so, but the question that interested Gullivan was, What can the individual learn and what can the interconnected individuals, the particular social system learn, what can be learned in Macromol, and more importantly what cannot (as it is) be learned. To answer this question he first had to trace the history – the history of conversations in Macromol up to the present. Secondly, he had to address the question of what is conserved, and thus, what can and cannot change. He then had to connect these factors to the individual or collective self-interest, that is what do they want to learn and why. What are the essential variables, the parameters of the future memory that trigger the selection of behavior, from the set of all possible behaviors? Indeed what can, cannot be discussed in Macromol?

History of Ideas in Good Currency in Macromol

If it's not paradoxical, it's not true. – Shunryu Suzuki

We only decide the undecidables. – Heinz von Foerster

*Solving a dilemma within its frame of distinctions
is akin to measuring gallons by the yard.*

As Gullivan returned from his long journey into unfamiliar conversations in not-Macromol, he reflected on the changes going on in Macromol from the 80's to the 90's and what unfolded in the 90's. As noted before during the 80's, there were two classes of conversations, one by those who had memories of the Red Phase in the 50's and the Yellow Phase in the 60's, who wanted to discuss the future space of possibilities, who had a visceral understanding of the devolving state of affairs in Macromol, and the other class of conversations centered on the processes of the here and now, mostly promoted by the more recent inhabitants of Macromol.

During the mid-80's, a small group of Technicals developed a story dealing with the macro principles of economic growth, the status and future prospects for growth in Macromol. This story was presented to the Cardinals, and widely discussed at several meetings. A team was chartered to more fully explore the potential discovery spaces in the new technologies of information, biotechnology and new materials, and their potential relevance to Macromol, and "what should we do." During the latter part of the 80's, the two classes of conversation, the new strategic direction advocates and the business process advocates met, and after many days of intense meetings, the forces for focus on process prevailed. The process advocates, mostly people without a technical background, saw the "solution" to the "future" economic well-being in Macromol as a matter of optimizing the existing pieces, a matter of motivation and alignment. They saw it in the then fashionable language of organizational effectiveness. Regeneration or renewal was cast as just one component of strategy, and since regeneration involved complex technical language, indeed new language to many, this complexity was dismissed and successfully marginalized. It was by now politically correct to focus on process organizational effectiveness. After two years of record earnings, the advocates of process had little doubt as to the merits of their position.

In the late 80's, a new Prince was selected by others to lead the island. The new Prince declared that the glory days of Macromol were over, thus the new "truth." Nobody asked the question, "What are the 'conditions of possibility' such that the glory days could return?" This question became unaskable because we had moved to a climate of mythic leadership. Now mythic leadership arises in exhausted social systems, inasmuch as it is the ideal discourse to create and conserve power. In mythic leadership the only reality is that which "I have created," reality is the meaning given to experience by symbolization. No basic laws, such as economic potential, determine what is possible. Causality is will and intentionality; change, regeneration is a matter of leadership; there are no criteria for action. Responsibility in mythic leadership becomes diffuse and even questionable, the mythic is amoral, and is not constrained by moral issues. There were, indeed, at this time, widespread discussions about responsibility without accountability, Gullivan remembers them well. There were many public speeches about valuing people, empowerment, the need to innovate, to continuously improve, to be more creative. The mythic leadership exhortations, the publicly self-validation of the importance of leadership, made it ever more clear that the leader was the source of power. It's a matter of will; you can be all you want to be. The future was cast in the goal of 4% real (accounting for inflation) growth. This was considered a strategy, a wish without a method to achieve the wish. Dwindling attempts to discuss necessary conditions that must exist to achieve the 4% real growth were dismissed in the common manner of "the Cardinal won't buy that." This phenomenon I call the fundamental error of confusing the play with the players. For Olivier to perform Hamlet, he first needed Shakespeare to write Hamlet. There is the common political process of dismissing what one does not understand, the content, by declaring that another will not accept the content, thus the dismissor relieves himself of the anxiety, the bio-cost of "having to" understand the content. The dismissor does not ask, "Let us first understand the content and then let us discuss an entirely *different* class of problem, how do we *convince* another?" The second problem is a problem of performance, not content.

With the economic downturn at the beginning of the 90's, the level of anxiety rose, and more and more inhabitants were encouraged to leave the island of Macromol. The mythic leadership culture grew stronger. The Prince assembled his Cardinals and Courtesans at faraway places, in the mythic spaces in the desert, and led the group to believe in the will to a bright future, the leadership team now became the Epic Team. Beneath the Epic rhetoric there lay the harsh financial realities – it was time to cut costs once again to become more efficient, process by process. The Prince then gave an edict that the activities on the island were to be broken down into self-contained subsystems, each with its own profit/loss responsibility. Once again, it was time for restructuring, for moving offices, for "cutting out the fat." Although this restructuring, sale of social assets, naturally improved the appearance of current surplus (though in reality a transfer of assets), in Gullivan's view, it radically hastened the devolution of the island, by the closing of the spaces of possible conversation. Each new subsystem spoke a more and more specific language, became more socially isolated, focused internally, and lost touch with the general community in Macromol. There was little space left for new generative conversations, and indeed, this shrinking space itself was isolated.

By the early 90's Gullivan had developed a good understanding of the changing mode of productivity in the general economy. Productivity gains up to the 70's and early 80's were primarily based on the decreasing cost of a unit of work, which started with the industrial revolution, and evolved through many physical and social structure changes. The basic business model, of transforming disordered inputs into high value ordered outputs, dealt with uncertainty of demand throughout the production and distribution chain by retaining "excess" stuff/energy at successive points along the chain. With the arrival of information technology, the mode of productivity began to shift to decreasing the cost of reducing uncertainty, uncertainty in demand, production, capital costs and allocation. The old business model, by its very structure, could not take full advantage of this new abundant resource, a necessary condition to be evolutionary current, thus viable. In 1992, the Jester put together about a two-hour presentation on these ideas, their consequences, and the need to restructure business models. He called his presentation The New Economy. Although the ideas were well received by many Cardinals, Courtesans, and Chiefs, they could not see how to incorporate them into their ongoing business activities and plans. They were too revolutionary and there was no energy to develop methods to get to new business models. One's career did not depend on long-term strategic change, it depended on calm attention to the present; after all, and the Prince had a blueprint for the future.

Throughout the 90's the population declined, the office relocations increased, the charts explaining the past got fancier, the struggle to hold onto jobs, status, future prospects intensified.

The Jester remembers an occasion where he made a presentation to the leading Technical group, all of whom had long distinguished careers in some specific technical area. Before he spoke there was a presentation on a new roofing material. As he listened to the presentation, it occurred to him that the whole business could be reframed in the context of the declining costs of communication and computation. He said why not "own" the problem, guarantee roof performance. Through the use of sensors, feedback and the appropriate network, this is now entirely possible. The market space expands by ten times or more and the research can focus on improving productivity within it. There were many blank stares. The Jester then presented his own ideas on economic potential and emerging technologies; however, this seemed to make the Technical audience uneasy and seemingly anxious to get it over with. This puzzled the Jester at first, as he had expected this group to be curious by nature. Then, as he reflected on the day's events, it dawned on him that they had a very strong interest in conserving their own conversation, their own special knowledge. He concluded that regenerative change does not arise from the "research" community. The research community is perhaps the most dynamically conservative group in Macromol. This community is, after all, constrained by its past and the language the Cardinals and the Prince will, in the technical perspective, understand. They, like others in Macromol, compete within their own social subsystem, even though the discourse is about the competition with those outside Macromol. The only true external competition is the competition between Princes.

As the 90's progressed, all attempts at strategic change were nullified, energies were focused on efficiency, "Six Sigma," devolution accelerated. A new Prince was in place, a Prince who had been mentored and nurtured by the mythic Prince for over two decades. The Jester's mentors, who so generously and vigorously supported him through the 90's, had by now all retired.

A living system, a system that can learn, evolve, adapt for the better has, as Ashby points out, a double feedback loop in its structural coupling with its environment. The "behavior" of the system, as the observer sees that it learns or adapts, reflects the selection of a behavior from a set of possible behaviors that are constrained by a set of essential variables, such that these essential variables are maintained within specific limits as defined by that living system, e.g., for us individually such limiting factors as blood pressure, blood glucose, blood carbon dioxide, etc. No behavior that results in the system going out of limits is "allowed" inasmuch as the system would no longer be that live system if such an event occurred. In Maturana's terms, the system can change its structure, its specific configuration in order to retain the essential relations between the subsystems – its organization. Failure to retain these essential relations results in the demise of the organization as such.

Now said Gullivan, "Let's look at social systems in general and then Macromol in particular." It seems intuitively obvious that *Design for a Brain* is isomorphic to "Design of a Social System." Every living system – a living entity in relationship to its environment – evolves in the same way: The previously successful systems that fail to learn and adapt are eliminated. It is not a matter of "survival of the fittest," but "survival of the good enough," or, more correctly, "elimination of the not fit enough." For humans – Homo sapiens sapiens, as Maturana would distinguish us – the ways we formulate our world, behave, and manipulate the environment in language are all subject to the law of natural selection. This includes corporations as a dominant class of modern social organization with enormous impact on the global economy and environment, and, inevitably, our everyday lives.

In a social system such as a corporation, the relevant environment is the historically-evolved and agreed-upon system of values, beliefs, social structures, norms, and rituals enacted in its language. This is the relevant environment because that which is conserved is what the organization is. It is clear that the medium of behavior in social systems, including corporations, is language rather than the physical world, because language is the medium of the agreements and transactions that constitute the forward motion of a corporation in its own terms (the natural sequence of discuss, agree, act, e.g., invest or carry out instructions). When measured by its executives or its stockholders, or in terms of offices and buildings or in any physical space whatsoever, these so-called material assets of the corporation only have meaning in discourse.

As Ashby says, the way for systems to achieve viability is to reach equilibrium with the environment. In social systems, the route to equilibrium for the individual is the process of gaining agreement. An error can only be recognized as such within the context and constraints of the local language. For example, you are not guilty until the judge and jury say you are guilty.

What does "survival" mean for the individual in the social context of the corporation? Further, what constitutes success? Promotion and salary increases are the foundation of recognition, presumably as a sign of contribution to the economic health of the organization (although they need not actually reflect that). Increased influence can be a factor for some individuals, in some circumstances. What constitutes failure? Loss of influence, demotion, losing the job entirely by being fired. In sum, for the individual in that social system, the social essential variables are those that pertain to social status, identity, the manner of making a living, and, in general, personal social security – that is, "being OK" as Homo sapiens sapiens.

"Detection and correction of errors," to invoke the common first-order cybernetic phrase, is, as usual, the prerequisite to achieving equilibrium. But in the current language of the individual, what can be detected? Errors can be of two types: first order errors, where adjustments must be made within the current discourse to maintain the (social) essential variables – the kitten adjusting its distance from the fire, or the company adjusting some interaction with customers and partners to improve inventory control. The current language is capable of expressing these errors, and changes to behavior can be made with positive effect. But what of the second-order errors, where a step-change, a different class of behaviors, is required to survive, and the current language is not capable of expressing the error? When new errors fall outside the local limitations of language, the social system is at risk. The corporation is doing the wrong things, its version of the truth is faulty, and the individuals inside the corporation "don't know that they don't know." They have a faulty theory of the world and can't possibly discus it.

Now, if we look at Macromol as the complex living system, a social system, the question then arises, what are we trying to conserve? What are the social essential variables? Gullivan said that all we need is to be reasonably accurate, illustrative, and that precision and comprehensiveness were less important at this juncture. Thus he decided that the three significant "factors," social essential variables that were conserved over the decades, the 50's to the late 90's were:

1. The aristocratic nature of the social hierarchy
2. The projection of a positive future surplus
3. A series of ritual behaviors that defined aristocratic social relations.

In the social hierarchy there were 16 levels of status, of importance. At the lower levels one moved up in half steps. The importance of these levels was manifest in office size, grandeur, isolation, access, and of course, who talks to whom and about what. Considerable significance was attached to small differences, mid-half-level differences by office windows, no windows, one or two windows, whether the office was 12' or 14' wide. Much discussion, debate, agreement proceeded the elevation of an inhabitant from one half level to the next. However, what characterized the social system as aristocratic to Gullivan was the major distinction between the levels of tribal chiefs and that of the Courtiers and the Cardinals. The selection process involved prior to admitting a new member to the court was very extensive. At first Gullivan assumed that experience, competence, and history of successful performance were criteria for admittance or selection to membership to the court. As time passed from the Red to the Blue Phase, it became clearer that Macromol was not a meritocracy. Social factors, including physical appearance, deference to ones "superiors," loyalty, appropriate Macromol manners, and above all, the belief

ABSTRACT

In this thesis, I use recent advance in statistics and econometrics in an effort to re-test some well-known theoretical propositions, examine whether those new techniques support the theory, provide models that are better fitted to describe and forecast economic time-series. The Purchasing Power Parity theory is tested using the Fisher and Seater (1993) and King and Watson (1997) methodologies and strong evidence in support of PPP is found. I use the general class of ARCH/GARCH processes to model financial time series in an ARIMA framework and the best fitted models outperform traditional ARIMA models in terms of the forecast variance. Finally, I test the balanced growth theory and try to estimate a money demand function using the Johansen and Juselius (1993) methodology. I do not find evidence in support of the balanced growth theory and a stable money demand function, and these results are not sensitive to different monetary aggregates that are constructed according to recent index number theory.

A thesis submitted to the faculty of graduate studies in partial fulfillment of the requirements for the Degree of Doctor of Philosophy

Department of Economics
University of Calgary
Calgary, Alberta
June, 2000
© Periklis Gogas 2000

ISBN 978-1-312-75014-2

90000

9 781312 750142

or, at least, expressed belief in the all-knowing wisdom of the Prince. People who might appear to challenge the aristocratic order either in social mores or expressed strategy were conspicuously excluded. Indeed, the essence of the social order could be felt or understood by paying attention to the special grooming classes, and indeed sometimes specific remedial grooming classes that potential members to the court passed through. The court was special, and conservation of the aristocratic court was central to life in Macromol.

There was the need to present a happy face to the market, to convince the market that surpluses in the short term would meet expectations and, of course, longer-term surpluses could be even greater. Projections about longer-term surpluses were characteristically optimistic. It was not necessary to explain in any rigorous way what had to be done to achieve these surpluses, or indeed if the path being followed could in principle lead to the promised surpluses.

The method of achieving the somewhat accountable short-term surpluses was particularly interesting to Gullivan. What interested him was how it was discussed on the one hand and not discussed on the other hand. Following the year 1975, a year of negative surplus, it became less and less possible to compose the necessary statement of near-term surplus to the market through the usual story of sales expansion, new products, technologically-based productivity gains. It became, as time progressed, necessary to sell assets. Now this sale of "people" assets was described as improvement in productivity and such metaphors as "cutting out the fat" were commonly used. There was, however, simply a reduction in the number of inhabitants on the island; there weren't enough valid jobs to go around. This, of course, was at least partially a result of difficult economic times at large, but more particularly it was a function of the contracting economic potential inherent in the specific activities and conversations current in Macromol. The "excess" social structure, which reflected considerable prior investment, was, to his way of thinking, sold off. What impressed him about this sale of assets was the way in which this perspective was hidden, not discussed even in the market. This sale showed up as surplus, i.e., it was a move of assets to current surplus, a way indeed of returning the investor's investment back to the owners of the island. With sleight of hand, all except the leaving inhabitants felt good. The significance of the sale of social structure as a powerful indication of the future prospects for growth in surplus from intrinsically or potentially more productive activities was somehow either not obvious or camouflaged.

In the ensuing decades some Princes took pride in generating current surpluses through sale of social assets, in achieving great efficiencies in believing that they increased the value of ownership through their efforts. The fact that they were achieving those results through the sale of social structure assets never entered the conversation. The failure to create new spaces of possibilities, new productive work, was not discussed, but more important, why this was so, was at best, barely discussed and, in Gullivan's view, poorly understood. This, of course, can easily be understood if one recognizes that, in the now, making a statement about near term surpluses, above a market expected limit, is an essential variable; it is conserved, and by whatever means is necessary, it and the aristocratic nature of the social system will be or is conserved.

Rituals are important in all social systems; indeed, the rituals we find ourselves performing on a regular basis reflect who we are and what we, silently at times, believe. Rituals are indeed the mechanisms by which other essential variables are conserved, so conservation of the mechanisms follows. There is a very extensive literature on the role of rituals in the domains of religion, the court, politics, etc., but Gullivan found little reference to the role of ritual in economic systems such as Macromol. In Macromol one very powerful ritual is the "safety meeting." He would say that all inhabitants of Macromol come to have a deep awareness of both on-the-job and personal safety, an asset of considerable value. Other rituals such as weekly, monthly reports, staff meeting, personal evaluations, etc. all have their own code, procedures, the rules are followed, the procedures enacted on an ongoing and regular basis. These rituals and the relation of power in the aristocracy, manifest and make possible, in the words of Foucault, the technology of power, the way in which the truth, the strategic conversation is constructed. Gullivan will discuss this central subject in greater detail later.

So Gullivan began to think of what is possible, what can change, by paying attention to and explaining why, what cannot change cannot change. Gullivan knew that he could spend a lot of time on essential variables, perhaps get lost in that domain, but he moved on with the conviction that he had "sufficient essential variable structure" to explore the domain of change. Is there some way to bring about appropriate change by design?

The Long Historical Conversation about Change

Cats don't bark.

The subject of change has been discussed, written about as far back as recorded history. The *I Ching*, the book of changes, reflects the cyclical view of all change: the flower emerges from the soil, grows and dies; and if one consults the oracle, the book of changes, or perhaps more appropriately if one interacts with the book of changes one can discover one's options. The Eastern notion of change is never one-dimensional, it is cyclical. The idea of absolute immobility is a non-conceivable abstraction. There is, however, the notion of non-change, but this refers to enduring social rituals, relationships; then there is sequential change, which is used to describe the succession of generations, not the more proximate lineal Western notion of cause and effect.

Our Western notion of change appears to be most rooted in proximate cause and effect, the four causes of Aristotle. The first cause corresponds to the form something is to become or to take, the acorn to the oak, the formal cause. The second is the material cause, the stuff the thing is made of. The third cause is the efficient cause, the *how* of the process, and then the final cause, why or for what purpose "it" was made. Other Greeks such as Heraclitus took the position that change is all there is, but Xenophanes took the position that nothing changes, change is an illusion, the parts might change but the whole (cosmos) is unchanging. From these and many other ideas over the centuries our concepts of change evolved. The Buddha noted that there is no substance, only form, and that all compound things decay, so form arises and decays in a never-ending cycle. This notion is not at odds with modern quantum physics and the conservation of energy, and, indeed, is none other than $E = mc2$ in motion.

In more recent times with the somewhat coterminous development of thermodynamics (the science of heat, energy, and work) and the geology of Charles Lyell, Darwin's work on natural selection, the industrial age in general, the ideas of progress, discussions of change took on an increasingly man-centric bias; man is the measure of all things, how could he change things for the better. The modern scientific stance led to a narrowing, a focusing on changing things, economies and even people for the better. By the 60's we had literally hundreds of books on how to change oneself, our social system, one's political system, but often little or any reflection on the consequences of these proposed changes. So Gullivan thought about how to look at change and what puzzles about change to solve. Gullivan said that when he thought about change, he was mostly interested in what was possible or not possible in principle. He was interested, he said, in the different kinds of change, distinctions he found useful. He also emphasized that he tended to focus on the rate of change, acceleration or deceleration as opposed to just linear change. Some factors may be increasing, but if you look at the change in the rate of change you can often see that that which appears to be growing is about to decline, collapse or die.

Gullivan said he was struck by the fact that in all these recent books on change there was little or no discussion on what change was, and an underlying assumption that all types of change were the same, indeed change was just change. The science of thermodynamics is based on the everyday observation that while a glass of hot water cools down, a glass of cold water does not naturally get hot. This one-way change, this irreversible change is in a sense the "arrow of time." Change is irreversible, you can't put your foot in the same river twice – the river and your foot change. The mechanism of evolution, natural selection, the one-way direction in evolution as discovered, or perhaps invented, by Darwin and Wallace led Gullivan to think about change in terms of evolutionary theory. In his book, *Selection, the Mechanism of Evolution*, Graham Bell summarizes the set of general principles that govern evolution through natural selection.

Heritable variation in the *rate of replication* causes (explains) evolution through selection. Heritable variation arises as *random* or *undirected* alterations of the nucleotide sequence, it does not in itself direct the course of evolution. The *rate of replication* is the only attribute that is selected directly. Characters that cause changes in the rate of replication will be selected indirectly and may evolve as a consequence. Adaptation caused by selection *in given conditions* is likely to be associated with *loss of adaptation* in other conditions. Evolution proceeds through the *sequential substitution* of superior variants, not exclusively by sorting pre-existing variation. A given state can evolve from a prior state only if the two states are connected by a *continuous series of slight modifications*, each of which is individually advantageous. Selection causes the modification of prior states of organization but *cannot abruptly give rise to wholly novel states*; the course of evolution is a historically unique contingent process conditioned by the fortuitous occurrence of particular variants. Selection *tends to improve performance in given conditions*, but does not always, and may never, optimize performance. Because selection is caused by differences in rate of replication, the outcome of selection will often depend on *what kind of competitors* are present, rather than on physical conditions of growth.

The way that these general laws mold the evolution of living organisms will be modulated by the developmental, physiological, genetic and ecological circumstances in which they operate. There is, indeed, a surprising resemblance between the above principles and what we observe in everyday economics. But of course, why not? We are just referring to the same events whether we describe them in the language of biology or economics. Many books have been written on this subject; however, Gullivan said he did not want to get into the nonproductive quagmire of trying to directly map one historical language with "its" purposes on to another which has an interest in explaining different aspects of the same thing. The biologists and the economists make their living in their own ways and belong to different languaging tribes.

The evolutionary changes in economics were noted by Schumpeter, Mensch and many others, but the failure to replicate, or the slowdown (in replication) by certain processes or organizations to create surpluses, versus new variants which replicated faster was not highlighted, creative destruction of capital was described but not explained in principle.

Thermodynamics first dealt with ideal isolated systems and how those systems behaved as they approached equilibrium. In the early part of the twentieth century, Onsager advanced the science to near equilibrium "stable" systems, but a major advance was made later by Prigogine when he developed the theoretical basis for explaining what happens in open systems far from equilibrium, the ultra-stable states as described by Ashby and noted earlier. Now these living systems achieve order, or ultra-stability, by the relationship between their particular structure, internal relationships, and the energy that passes through them, as open systems. These systems "use" energy (order, or high-quality energy) to create internal order or structure to degrade high quality energy, dissipate energy, create waste, and grow (within limits) in the process.

The plants use the energy of the sun, the chicken eats the seeds from the plants, we, of course, eat the chickens, and indeed the more advanced our economy, the more efficiently (from a thermodynamic perspective) we degrade the sun's energy and the more waste we produce. Now an interesting thermodynamic aspect of an open system far from equilibrium is that when the system gets unstable, beyond a certain point, it either dies or it splits off into a new phase or set of phases. The species either dies or gives rise to a new species, or provides space for a different species, with a different lineage, to thrive, replicate, replace. What is important here is that to correct an error, an error that threatens survivability beyond the bifurcation or speciation point, one, in principle, would have to go back to the state before the speciation or bifurcation event; however, this is not permissible, since these changes are irreversible. You cannot go home, you cannot reinvent the past. It is extraordinary how many times Gullivan had seen great plans to "fix the business" with the idea that once fixed, the business could successfully move forward. This is where the naive notion of change leads to semantic confusion, wishful thinking and the high cost of ignorance. You can't reinvent a business with an economic potential close to 1, close to equilibrium, however comforting it is to think so.

So from biology and thermodynamic perspectives we have an understanding of irreversible change and the distinction between evolutionary change, phase change, developmental change or change in the system in the same phase.

The next language system that Gullivan wanted to look at to explain the same change or types of change is language itself. A new idea, a new distinction is, on some possibly random basis, uttered by someone to someone. A listener "understands" and so the idea gains currency. This is how Gullivan describes invention: invention is the opening of a semantic space, the introduction of new distinctions, new conversations are now possible. But as noted in evolutionary biology these "ideas" have histories and are fusions (in the Pask sense) of two previous ideas (or conversations). "I hold the idea," Gullivan said, "that nothing comes from nothing and there are no historical or spontaneous new life forms or new ideas."

With invention, the opening of the new semantic space, the space of possibilities or new conversations, can proceed or can develop from this invention. This space Gullivan called the discovery space in knowledge or economic activity, science. Developmental biology deals with the journey of the fertilized egg along its unique history, with all its possibilities as it is structurally coupled to its environment, and this process is isomorphic with discovery, the process of conversation, creating further distinctions and their associated behaviors.

So we have the change at what Gullivan, for simplicity, calls Level I – invention, its random nature – and change at Level II – discovery of what is now possible, discussable, its growth or expansion, the formulation of language, processes, procedures, "competence", social structure – which leads to the possibility of change at Level III. Change at this level is about improvements on a daily basis, repetition, skill development; in other words, it's about efficiency. The most important aspect of these three levels is I must precede II and II must precede III. No amount of efficiency can lead to discovery and no amount of discovery can lead to invention (as I use these words), said Gullivan.

This same structure, from invention to efficiency, from species change to solving everyday problems, also exists in basic science. Though Newton formulated the law of gravity, it is a source law. It says that when two objects, of such and such a mass are separated by a distance they will attract each other, with a given force according to the law of gravity. It is worth noting here that the earth does not have gravity, there is no absolute anything, one cannot detect absolute motion, and gravity arises in the relationship between two bodies. But what is gravity? Now Gregory Bateson would describe gravity as an explanation, an explanation to explain anything you want, the mapping of a description onto a tautology, to give an explanation, an explanatory principle. Bateson looks at gravity in the context of our languaging. But what is gravity physically? Well nobody knows, we accept it and proceed from there. We proceed to consequence laws, such as *force is equal to mass times acceleration* and from there we can design such things as ordnance, cannons, etc. In the science of electrodynamics we start with another source law, Coulomb's Law; now what are Coulombic forces? We don't know, but once again, based on everyday observation, we start there and proceed to develop the consequence laws and then everyday practical applications. But back to biology and evolutionary theory, unlike scientific laws, the concept of fitness is conceptually different, it's a supervening property that is a relationship between a given organism and its particular environment, that is, it is a property specific to each case, unlike Newton's second law of motion, Force equals mass times acceleration ($F = ma$), which is general to all relevant cases.

Now the reason that Gullivan found this important is that many people in the social sciences, economics and business consider the methods, language, and explanatory systems of science appropriate to deal with "social problems." That, Gullivan thought, was a fundamental error. The error is rooted in the mythology of objectivity, the primary myth in the Western cultures. In objective mythology there are objective facts, right and wrong ways of arguing, all indeed highly useful in the sciences, engineering, etc. where agreement can be reached, based on shared assumptions which can usually be made quite explicit. In biology, which Gullivan liked to call the social domain, while rejecting the premise that there is a social science. In social systems, different explanatory systems are appropriate which take historical factors, self-interest, language, agreement, determinacy, structure, structural coupling, and indeed, what one can know into account. Some might see the latter explanatory system as close to subjectivism, the older mythology. However, let's ask the question, how do we become subjects? I think, therefore I am not alone; one cannot, as Wittgenstein says, have a private language, reality; even one's own "subjectivity" is a social construct. Misapplied comfortable objectivity so very often leads to unwise use of resources, unwise use of power, and unreasonable claims to possessing the truth, with all its attendant consequences. So Gullivan wondered, what is the truth, where does it come from, what are we to believe? Now that we can see that there are different kinds of changes, and in everyday life changes are irreversible, follow an evolutionary path as distinct from, say physics, where time past is not distinguished from time future, and that we must very carefully choose our systems of explanations to get what we want, how we can come to agree on the "right" course of action, to adapt for the better.

Before discussing what he discovered about the truth, how it comes about, Gullivan returned to that class of change he called efficiency. Now what system of explanation should he use to arrive at a comfortable understanding of efficiency? Well, this took him quite a while. He moved on from the usual engineering, structural or financial languages; these objective measures, which in most cases reflected the past and gave us a comfortable feeling of being in control, of having the ability to make decisions, of being rational, advance our career, and indeed, often write impressive reports or books. While these objective measures are often very useful, very comfortable, he was looking for some way of explaining how these "behaviors" come about. Why do we place such faith in these measures, why do we spend such vast efforts in the pursuit of these measures? Why is it that the worse things seem to be getting, the more we resort to measurement, the daily exhortation to cut costs, be more efficient? So what is the biological nature of efficiency?

The Dark Side of Efficiency

Some people add, some add up.

From his historical perspective, which included his conversation with Pask, Maturana and many others, and the ideas discussed above, Gullivan began to study information theory from the perspective of objective science, as in Pierce, *An Introduction to Information Theory*, and Gregory Bateson as in *Communication* by Ruesch and Bateson.

In Chapter 8, Gregory Bateson writes about the relationship between validity and belief. To quote, "Man lives by those propositions whose validity is a function of his/her belief in them." A cat is a cat because we both agree that this is so. When two people are communicating, the events in their environment, and in their not-nervous system, trigger events in the nervous system. These latter events are coded in some manner so that communication can take place. With a shared history of communication there is little noise and a high degree of mutual understanding. The codification is necessarily systematic; otherwise the triggers would be interpreted as noise. Lacking a shared history, a history of shared values, and agreements, communication becomes difficult, misunderstandings rise, noise rises and the conversation gives rise to stress and anxiety. Consequently, the participants in a very difficult or impossible conversation shift their attention to events that result in a less stressful internal state.

The historically arrived at value system, the system of codification is in a real sense a set of preferences, by which certain "messages" are selected in and other "messages" are tuned out. Those messages that are tuned out fade into the background, they are dismissed, and they are left undefined and unexplained. Our system of values determines what we see or hear, or pay attention to, so we act according to how we wish to see or hear, or how the world is known to us. This system of values, codification is conserved, to maintain "ultrastability" to avoid the pain or frustration of inner conflicts. We see this every day when two opposing political candidates interpret the "facts" entirely differently. The "facts" are arranged according to the value system in such a way that the observer gets back to where the observer was, i.e., the comfortable state. Facts are only facts according to some theory, some system of codification some value system, indeed, to some local agreement. They do not exist outside language. The degree to which the value system, the codification system, is conserved can be illuminated by empathizing with the angst the "priest" suffers when he loses his faith in his God.

In Macromol, it is clear that the members of the court – the Prince, the Cardinals and the Courtiers – have a long history of shared values, shared systems of codification and, consequently, they will tend to agree on what is a fact, what should be measured, and indeed, most importantly, what is an error, what needs to be fixed. Why, one might ask, should a Cardinal talk about a new opportunity foreign to the court, requiring a new system of explanations, a new way of seeing, when he runs the risk of being viewed as talking noise? What appears to be decision-making in the court can be seen as the non-conscious process of discussing the familiar, the understandable, making adjustments in the context of the comfortable, the familiar, and arriving at the conclusion that a decision has been made. Whether one believes that one makes a decision, or that one acts according to one's history in a given context, and the "decision making process" is just a description of the decider, is important. The belief in "making a decision" truncates the process of self-discovery and thus greatly diminishes the probability of seeing from a new perspective, or even recognizing that there are other perspectives. The belief in "making a decision" also leads to the belief that "they know" what they are doing, just trust them. The lure of this position is obvious; one can at least have the comfort of clarity without having to deal with the awkward question of validity.

First, as Gullivan said, with the aristocratic value system, the social status is conserved as mentioned above; the people in Macromol will respond to the social status cues and will in their own self-interest guide their messages accordingly, and will attempt to send only those messages that he or she expects to be favorably received. Secondly, if we look at the history of a member of the court – the history of conversation, agreements that met the necessary and sufficient conditions that led to the series of promotions to the rank of the court – then we can claim that the set of possible conversations that the members will engage in is constrained by that history and the conservation of aristocratic values. Thus, we can claim that the constrained conversation and agreements constrain the set of possible strategies that can be formulated and accepted to deal with today's and tomorrow's possibilities. These strategies are in a sense selected for automatic success (or failure, if too novel) inasmuch as the goals are limited by what can be discussed. Then how can the people learn such that they can successfully engage in new domains of possibility if, indeed, they cannot, or do not want to, hear or discuss them.

Management is a conservative function and although it, in its own interest, speaks loudly and often about change, the need for innovation, its integral structure is such that it is adversarial to such uncertainty. The drive for efficiency as constrained by the historical conversation is such that significantly new conversations are unlikely, unwelcome, and indeed, as the stress level rises, survival for the individual requires that he or she constrain their conversation so that they fit the accepted view of reality. Gullivan asked why efficiency as a goal, indeed as a theory of business, seems to crowd out new conversation and new possibilities? Could it be that a previously successful social group, an island, is doomed to extinction by virtue of the history of success itself and the constraints on the system that inevitably arise from that success? Why can't, or what must happen, for a social system to go from success to success?

Let us, Gullivan said, go back to the Red Phase discussed earlier and think about the learning curve, the increasing efficiency, the rising profits and see what happened in those periods from the point of view of what was discussable, what agreements and what strategies were possible. To explain his point of view, Gullivan needed to introduce Shannon's work on information theory. The work of Shannon and Bateson is highly complementary. Bateson focused on values, meaning, codification, learning, learning to learn, the very nature of human communication, what it was and what it was not. Shannon, on the other hand, addressed the question of how to send/receive messages efficiently, and in his particular case, messages sent over the telephone wires, regardless of the content or meaning of the message. So let's look at efficiency from the Shannon perspective, while keeping the Bateson perspective in mind.

When Morse code was invented, it is interesting to note that Morse did not just arbitrarily assign dots or dashes or pauses to just any letter. He visited the printer's shop to see how many blocks of each letter the printer found from experience he needed. For example, he found that E was the most common letter, so he assigned a single dot to E and proceeded to assign the simplest set of dots and dashes to the letters according to the printer's experience of their use. In other words, Morse was not only concerned with telegraphy, sending messages, but also efficient messaging. In fact, he was within 15% of the theoretical maximum. From Morse's work in 1832 most of the effort to improve efficiency, over land lines and transatlantic cable was directed at solving the noise problems which distorted messages and was not surprisingly categorized as a "physics" problem.

Shannon reframed the problem and perhaps said to himself, "The problem is not how to deal with the signal and noise so as to get the most accurate and most efficient messaging, but how should I encode the message in the first place to meet the goal of accuracy and efficiency." Shannon turned to the English language and studied the frequency of letters, part words, words and words that follow other words, etc. Based on these everyday frequencies, and using binary code, i.e. ones and zeros, Shannon showed how the English language could be approximated by a mathematical process which could be executed by a machine. Shannon showed that by proper encoding you can send a message over a noisy channel with a negligible level of error. You could calculate how many characters (digital) you could send over a channel of a given band width per unit time with almost no error. He provided the semantic space in which extraordinary discoveries pertaining to communication have since been made.

Although Shannon's theory of communication is a mathematical theory, his work and way of thinking have had a profound influence in many domains, of course, communication, computation, but also language and meaning, cybernetics, psychology. The impact of Shannon's work on Gullivan's understanding of communication was mostly in the area of social systems. The value of a message is a function of the amount of uncertainty that it reduces for the receiver. In a conversation a particular sentence can be viewed as "information" and its value (surprise) understood in that it clarifies something for the receiver, that it reduces the listener's uncertainty. The amount of information one needs, as we note from our everyday experience, is related to the difficulty of the task, perhaps the time, attention, concentration needed to accomplish the task. In a biological perspective we might call this the *bio-cost*. We are all aware from our daily experiences that we have limitations: limitations on our energy, time, attention span, concentration, and more importantly, on our vocabulary. We economize on the use of these scarce or constraining resources. Many studies have shown that a decrease in familiarity with words in communication, and an increase in the number of syllables in those words, slows down the conversation process. Zipf's law indirectly points out how we favor more commonly used words, which Zipf associated with the principle of least resistance, or least effort. Our attention span is limited and Miller's law states that after a brief period of observation of, say familiar names or objects, a person can remember only 7 ± 2 such names or objects. We also know from our daily work that it takes a lot of effort to write a paper, prepare a speech. This is because we have to go from the random set of words we know to the ordered arrangement for the paper or speech, and as we noted above, going from disorder, the probable, to order, the improbable, is called work.

If we consider what we have discussed about communication and go back in time to the Red Phase in Macromol, we can readily understand that this discovery phase was, indeed, a time of creating new language, new distinctions. New technology always is, Gullivan claims, the creating of new language, new distinctions; otherwise the communications would be full of noise and ambiguity. As the new language became the familiar language, something interesting began to happen. Now that the language was familiar, the task was to make communication more efficient. It should be noted that all production, shipment, promotion and other such social actions are preceded by conversations. The machines don't run spontaneously; someone says, "Let's start the machine and make so much of so and so." So as the social system tries to be more efficient in communication (though not always aware of this), it reduces the vocabulary, and indeed, the number of syllables in the words, it makes frequent and increasing use of acronyms. This efficient communication is a necessary condition to create a more efficient physical production system. If this were not so, the capital cost of a new plant would be too high (competitively), it would appear too complex and would demand excessive time. Efficiency is a function of clarity of purpose, which requires clarity in communication.

Now enter the Orange Phase, and if an outsider were to sit in a staff meeting or read some of the business/technical communications, he or she would be confronted with much frustration because the language has now become "Macromol-speak," highly efficient and understandable within Macromol, but almost arcane outside the island. To illustrate the point, if I were to refer to the Krebs cycle in the domain of the biologist, it takes just two words to get my message across. However, if the conversation occurred with a group of business analysts, it would perhaps take me about 200 words to accomplish an understanding, i.e., two orders of magnitude in communication productivity.

So, as the social system in Macromol becomes more efficient, its language narrows the cost or perhaps the nature of efficiency. This factor has enormous future consequences, e.g., in the Green and Blue Phases, new business opportunities could not be mapped onto the now efficient narrow language, so those at the court with these histories were unable or reluctant to listen to new language, perhaps it appeared to them as noise. The drive to greater and greater efficiency is somewhat addictive. It has a kind of clarity that the fundamentalist knows. In biology, natural selection selects against the previously successful, the highly efficient in a previous environment. When the landscape changes, survival depends on plasticity, not efficiency. In Macromol, as it is in other islands, it is the language plasticity, what can be discussed, that determines survivability. In the Blue Phase, those in Macromol must now bring specific new strategies to bear on the business of making a living for its members. Those appropriate strategies are constrained by the general economy, technology, etc., i.e., the ecology and the history of the social system. Now Gullivan claimed that when there are major changes in the ecology, the appropriate strategies can be identified; however, the important strategic question is, "Can they be discussed?" These major changes reflect major changes in the distribution or abundance of resources. In the industrial age, including the late industrial age of chemistry, the abundant resource was energy. The cost of a unit of work (disorder to order) decreased dramatically as fossil fuels, efficient engines, and hydroelectric plants became ubiquitous. Powered machines replaced muscles. However, now we see a reduction in the cost of computation that facilitates the nervous system in its continuous task of reducing uncertainty. The strategy that is not based on generating its productivity from the new abundant resource is out of sync with the ecosystem. Success depends on auto-catalytically converting resources into organization, just as it did in the Red Phase in Macromol.

So, Gullivan said that Macromol, or its court, conserves the aristocratic system of governance, and its previous success was based on now old language, and its future success requires new language. Gullivan also noted that the Prince can hinder or facilitate future success, and this raised the question of power. Gullivan felt that he needed to address the role of power and the role of leadership, but before doing so, he restated the types or levels of change since what can be discussed flows irreversibly from (our class) one class of change to another, just as in evolution.

Change, the need for change, is visceral. I, or we, are not getting what we want. "I don't feel okay about my future security." Gullivan distinguished three embodied classes of change:

1. **The Act of Invention** – Opening a new semantic space

2. **Acts of Discovery** – Specific problem focus – Creation of new distinctions, new instructions – that is, language

3. **Acts to Increase Efficiency** – Processes and procedures, e.g., "six sigma" – Organizing people, machines, and communications to achieve lower cost per unit of output, narrowing the language

Each of three classes can be construed as the domain of an individual or a group, that is, each class is carried out by a different type of individual. This is because the belief system, the values, self-interest, and overt behavior of these three classes are quite different. For example, individuals focused on changes for efficiency have no "space" to consider the issues of invention. It is outside their style and focus, no less outside their language. Life-styles, "life meaning," the way in which they achieve satisfaction differs markedly. Once again, the genetic history is one form of learning that has impact on the tendency and capacity for exhibiting a particular class of change; and interaction with the environment (the ontogenesis) does the rest. It seems likely that Einstein, for example, was predisposed to Class 1. He would say that himself.

Notice that the flow goes from Class 1 to Class 2 to Class 3. As in evolution and developmental biology, entropy-change goes one way. You cannot go, in the same semantic space, from efficiency to discovery, much less invention. You cannot learn what you already know; you cannot invent what has already been invented. You cannot improve the productivity now by what you have done in the past, because of what has changed in the meantime.

Here are some examples of this flow of change from Class 1 to 2 to 3. In the 1960's, Carver Mead asked a key question: What are the limits of Very Large-Scale Integration (VLSI) – that is, how many computational elements can you get into a given area of silicon? What is the theoretical limit of the number of switches that can be packed into a single chip? This is change in form of Class 1, opening a new semantic space – beforehand, digital switches were implemented out of individual components. This new space in turn gave rise to a whole new set of questions – Class 2 – as how to approach the theoretical limit proposed by Mead. These questions constituted the birth of Silicon Valley, because answering these questions provided a roadmap for creating new, viable products. Finally, answering questions in Class 3 led to the progress measured by Moore's Law, a characterization of the pace at which the industry approaches Mead's theoretical calculation of the ultimate limit. One could go into further detail – for example, to show how Mead's original calculation implies the answer to questions in Class 2 – but that is not necessary to the present discussion.

Another example of these three classes of change starts in the early part of the twentieth century at Macromol – with the invention of means to selectively make and shape macro-molecules with chemical techniques. This opened up a conceptual space in which it was possible to conceive of natural materials being mimicked by composing synthetic materials out of combinations of long-chain molecules, thereby copying naturally occurring substances but hopefully also improving them – making them more comfortable, durable, malleable, etc. The invention of macromolecular chemistry constitutes the opening of a new semantic space that led in turn to, say, thousands of questions as to how to actually manipulate the materials predictably, requiring in turn the discovery of many thousands of answers. This gave rise to the creation of strong, super strong and elastic strings. Over time, improving the efficiency of manufacturing and product-creation processes meant that an existing business could continue to generate wealth for many years – so long as there was ignorance in the system whose removal constituted lower costs and, therefore, potential profit.

Of course, the biologist will recognize that evolutionary and developmental biology theory contains components that are isomorphic to the three classes of change, from invention to discovery to increased efficiency. When we talk about regenerative change, remember that we are talking about a change in the mode of productivity, where actions or "programs" will lead to a surplus. This surplus can be invested in the same space to produce further surplus, otherwise you are relatively less and less productive and will be "selected out."

"To me," Gullivan said, "leadership and power are two different concepts, although it is clear from our experiences that they are inexorably inter-twined. Leadership is about clear and valid messages which I will discuss later, power is about listening and selecting, executing and deciding on the distribution of surpluses. So how does power arise, where does it come from, and how is it manifested?"

About Leadership and Power

We have done it ourselves. – Lao-tse

Gullivan began by reflecting on the many books he had read over the years on power and its related manifestations. While he was still at school at Garbally, he read the usual Greek classics of Plato, Aristotle and their views on power and governance. He liked to read a lot about ancient Greek, Roman an Egyptian history, but most of the stories were about the King, Emperor or Pharaoh, their armies and their battles. Little was recorded about the everyday lives of the people and their relationship to the Sovereign. Plato and Confucius wrote a lot about ideal forms of government, but his favorite words were from Lao-tse:

Of the best of rulers, the people only know that they exist.

The next best they love and praise. The next they fear. And the next they revile.

When they do not command the people's faith, some will lose faith in them.

And then they resort to oaths. But of the best when their task is accomplished and their work done, the people all remark "We have done it ourselves."

But all this hearsay of the long distant past does not seem to fit Gullivan's experience today. However, four books about power and warfare still resonated with him. One he read at school, *Richelieu*, the story of how the Cardinal created what might be called the position of the first modern prime minister. The other three were, of course, the classics Sun Tzu, *The Art of War*, and von Clausewitz, *On War*, and Machiavelli, *The Prince*, all of which were in good currency at the business schools in the early days of deregulation, the early 80's. Once again, although it was the "in thing" to discuss these books in the mid-80's, they did not give Gullivan any real understanding as to what power was all about. He then discussed several personal incidents where he had experienced power "directly," sensing when he did and did not have "it." His first such experience was back in the 70's when he laid out a program, referred to earlier, to uncover the mysteries as to why we could not get conductive string to work to "eliminate" the static problem with mats.

The program, the work, was highly successful, but the Technical chief was not particularly pleased inasmuch as his theory of how it worked was disproved; technical success was, in fact, a "political" failure.

Over the next few years, there were other similar incidents. For example, Gullivan's position in the early 80's that oil prices would not rise as the prevailing wisdom had it. They would, according to his analysis, indeed, fall significantly during the 80's, an unpopular and career de-enhancing position. It was also common to hear phrases like, "He who holds the gold, holds the power." At a grand strategy meeting in the late 80's, a meeting that lasted a few days, a memorable incident occurred. At the end of the meeting, the presiding Cardinal summed up the meeting, and this was, of course, in the age of the mantra valuing people, the Cardinal noted that Gullivan was the only one the group "picked on," singled out for derogatory remarks. Then he added, "He has broad shoulders, he can handle it." This event was quite humiliating and disturbing to Gullivan – the outcast – but a day later it occurred to him that he had, perhaps by virtue of the kind of statements he made, a certain kind of power. Why were these people afraid of what he was saying and why did they feel the need to react? During this time it became increasingly clear to Gullivan that his journey was taking him further and further away from the comfort of old Macromol speak and, consequently, he must have appeared to be speaking a different language and trying to change the conversation in a direction that most of the inhabitants did not want to go. Hence the need to play the Jester more fully.

At a somewhat later date, one of the Courtiers had some misgivings about staying on the island. He thought perhaps that there were better opportunities elsewhere. Indeed, he had received an enticing offer from another island. He came to the Jester as a friend to discuss his "problem." What should he do? Somewhere during the discussion the Jester remarked to him, "But I have no power." "Oh, yes, you do," he replied. "Think about to whom you talk." The Jester thought about that later and noted that, indeed, he had unusual and private access to the Prince and many of the Cardinals. Perhaps that had something to do with power. Perhaps the key to understanding power lay in the language or the approach one took. In essence, what are the right tools to do the job, and how an inappropriate approach can be quite misleading. This led to an introduction of the work of Foucault.

Gullivan went to the library in Paris and had a long conversation with Michel Foucault. He discussed his problems and frustrations, what he had witnessed in Macromol and asked him to enlighten him about this mysterious topic – power in social systems. Foucault was born in 1926 in Poitiers, France, and grew up at a time when Sartre "existence before essence," existentialism, and Derrida with deconstruction and Barthes with semiotics. Foucault's former examiner, Georges Canguilhem, had undertaken the new fashionable approach, deconstruction, to the history of natural science, biology. Foucault was *very* interested in the work of Hegel, who sought to find meaning in history, and by Nietzsche's work on the philosophy of power, the will to power, and in the ideas of Heidegger, who was more inclined to see life as determined by more mundane factors than the fashionable idea of reason. Foucault sought to find out how reason, the thoughts, todays widely accepted beliefs actually came to be so. From whence did the present come? He decided not to explore such well-studied subjects as the hard sciences, but *took* as his subject madness, not just to record the events of the past, but to "illuminate the present." The present attitude to madness is a matter of agreement, social perception, social practice, where Foucault might have asked, when was madness separated from unmadness? Or more currently reason from unreason?

So Foucault began by asking, how did our ideas evolve? In the middle ages, the "mad" were considered blessed by God and often considered wise. But, following the Renaissance, the so-called age of reason began. Perhaps one could say it began with doubting of Descartes: "I think, therefore I am." But what if instead he had said, "I think, therefore we are." Perhaps western philosophy would not have had to wait another couple of centuries for Wittgenstein to lay bare philosophy as a semantic game. My approach, Foucault said, was that of an archeologist showing how the prevailing ideas of the day, the social conditions, the economic fortunes of the people and what might seem matter of pure chance shaped the course of what was considered the right thing to do, the right thing to talk about, what he called the episteme of the time. The episteme was what was discussable and, indeed, thinkable. Surely the voyage of Columbus was unthinkable when it was true that the earth was flat. For example, with the disappearance of leprosy in the 13th and 14th centuries in France and England, many large buildings became empty, so "what do we do now?" Slowly, and in this context, with the rise of reason, the idea of unreason, the asylum evolved. Along with the evolution of the asylum came the rest of the apparatus, psychiatry, psychology and the discourses belonging to their subjects and, of course, the rise in the social and legal authority of the psychiatrist. Foucault declared that he denied the teleology of history and sees it much as an evolutionary biologist might see it as a part of chance. The truth, the ideas in good currency, are subject to history and the mechanism of natural selection, it is essentially an agreement on what works now and, of course, now keeps changing.

This approach to the truth is reminiscent of Einstein's work. Time, he said, is not an invariant, time is local. Likewise, the "truth" is local in space and time, there is no invariant truth. Changes in technology such as machines or medicine are always associated with a shift in power. They are inextricably linked. Witness today as medical technology advances, the power of medicalization increases. The truth changes, and the central "truth" of the "normal" brings with it the drive to fix people to be normal.

Foucault said that his work on the evolution of our current common sense on madness led him to what was of great interest to Gullivan, the understanding of power, power/knowledge, what is the "truth." In his masterpiece, *The Order of Things*, which he discussed, Foucault traced the evolution of ideas, memes from the 17th century to the present version of the truth. At first he was difficult to understand, but in recursive conversations, Gullivan found that his perspective had changed, and what Foucault had to say became clearer and more relevant. Gullivan thought that, if possible, it was best to read and discuss Foucault's work through the lens of an evolutionary biologist, not to look at living entities in the usual way, but at what we humans do and believe as we evolve, the evolution of the discourses themselves and their consequences. Again, as in biology, life is the relationship between the "DNA" in the cell and the cell in the environment. To ask the question, "Is it nature of nurture?" is in Gullivan's view an illegitimate question. In the same sense, unlike Nietzsche's "Superman," Foucault saw power as that which exists in relation between people, and not a "thing" in itself, or indeed, not something that one possesses.

Perhaps the initial difficulty in understanding Foucault's ideas stems from the common challenge any student has in trying to understand or communicate a shift in perspective. The difficulty lies in the requirement to use the language of the day, with its distinction and definitions to say something quite different. The problem is not so much in being understood as the difficulty that arises in using the language of the day to avoid being misunderstood. So it takes desire and time to allow the change in perspective to become the new normal. It took the leading scientists of the day over five years to fully appreciate what Einstein had said about time, that it was not a universal invariant, but was local, a function of the local gravitational field; thus Einstein changed the truth. This point, of the necessary time, desire, and attention is important, inasmuch as the busy and somewhat successful "executive" is highly unlikely to make such a personal investment. Gullivan's desire to understand what Foucault was saying was driven by his initial feeling that his system of explanations, his perspective on power, was much more useful, productive in understanding how the world works than his previous perspective on power, truth and knowledge. His previous perspective was essentially the prevailing viewpoint, that of seeing power as being vested in the sovereign, the state, the wealthy, power as warfare, class struggle, power as negative, constraining, and most of all a "thing" some had and some did not have. "This negative viewpoint had little explanatory power," said Gullivan, and he considered it highly misleading and not useful.

Foucault said, I invert the maxim of von Clausewitz that war is politics continued by another means, to power is war continued by various other means. Of course, if one takes the ecological perspective, it is quite understandable. We all, in a sense, struggle and compete in order to make a living in an ever-changing environment. What results, as we enact our world, is always the result of a contest of strength, the outcome of competing self-interests. Power is exercised and created at the same time just like our production and transmission of electrical power. Power manifests itself in the rules of "right," who gets to decide what discourses will occur. There can be no exercise of power without the production, accumulation, circulation of discourses, what people discuss, pay attention to, and what rules and procedures are deemed acceptable. Who talks to whom and about what.

Power cannot be separated from the "truth," Foucault said, for, indeed, the exercise of power is the production of the truth. We are all in the process of producing, creating the truth. In order to function we must believe we speak the truth. We must produce truth as we must produce wealth; indeed, we must produce the truth in order to produce wealth. This drive to produce the truth in order to and as a means to produce wealth is easily seen in the development of technology. In R&D, progress is made by agreeing on what is "now" true. This is the basis for concerted action. As Foucault said, "We are destined to a mode of living as a function of true discourses which are the bearers of the specific effects of power," we are trapped in our own time. Sometimes we note, especially in retrospect, what appear to be changes in the truth, say in the sciences. What change are the rules of formation of statements, which are not considered acceptable within that particular culture, society of, say, a group of scientists, the internal regime of power. What was previously unthinkable, undiscussable, irrational, now becomes the new truth. So it appears in retrospect like a rational phase shift. Power pervades the entire society and makes possible the production of things, the production of knowledge (or a new class of knower), indeed, it, as Foucault says, induces pleasure, a key point missed by many previous teachers.

Truth and power coexist like electricity and light (bulb). Again, as Foucault said, "Truth is a thing of this world, it is produced only by virtue of the multiple forms of constraint and it induces regular effects of power." Each society has its own regime of truth, its general politics of truth, i.e., the type of discourse which it accepts and functions as true. The mechanisms and instances which enable one to distinguish true and false statements, the means by which each is sanctioned, the techniques and procedures accorded value in the acquisition of the truth, the status of those who are charged with saying what counts as true – these are the underpinnings of power. Truth is to be understood as a system-ordered procedure for the production, regulation, distribution, circulation and operation of statements. Truth is linked in a circular relation with systems of power which produce and sustain it, and the effect of power which it induces and which extends its regime of truth. Don't we fight every day for the truth? Indeed, truth/power defines, constrains, the conditions of possibility for the formation of certain forms of knowledge, actions, mode of living, as a function of time and place. It is an "historical *a priori*."

Foucault then discussed the distinction between the technology, programs, and strategy of power. With the rapid growth of the human sciences, (demographics, sociology, psychology, psychiatry, economics), the "technology" of power evolved, the technology to "manage" social systems, to exercise power efficiently to move from an "oppressive power" to a disciplinary power. The increasing general knowledge of acting in one's own self-interest, in matters of health, education, career, etc., moves us along the path of power/truth and self-discipline. But at the same time, the "desire" to be normal, normal in the new medical sense, may indeed bring about highly undesirable results. What is the future of the medicated children, the anxiously medicated adults and the technology to keep the very old very old? This is human technology, these are now ideas in good currency.

We live in a world of programs, social, medical, corporate. Programs usually have stated goals, and there is the assumption of the truth in the field of knowledge pertaining to the subject, the domain of intent or the domain of proposed action. The common axiom of programs is that an effective power is and must be a power which knows the object upon which it is exercised. Further, the condition that the programmatic knowledge must satisfy is that it renders reality in the form of an object which is programmable. The importance of programs lies not in their realization or their effectivity (since things rarely go as programmed), but in the condition of possibilities created by the discourse which are exercises of truth/power. The program creates conditions of possibility for the generation of knowledge. Those "inside" the program may be quite unaware of the spaces they are creating for new knowledge to evolve in quite unexpected areas. Think of prisons becoming a viable business! Foucault then defined strategy at the intersection of technology and programs as the exploitation of possibilities. What are the possibilities that arise out of the program discourse, its truth, the technology – a field of strategy? Thus, strategy is opportunistic in the Foucault sense, but in a sense perhaps this is a more valid description or explanation of what actually happens. Now Gullivan thought if this seemed really dense, switch to evolutionary theory, natural selection (elimination), think of memes in place of genes, the natural evolution, and selection of memes in the social system.

Lastly, Foucault discussed some important observations on the role of the intellectual, the writer, the author. The role of the intellectual has changed from the day of, say, Marx or Voltaire, where the intellectuals concerned themselves with what was "just and true for all." Today, in contrast, the intellectuals come from the laboratories, the universities, with specific knowledge. They deal with real material matters. For example, since World War II, the atomic scientists with their knowledge/ power, which could destroy life, became a matter of considerable political significance. Today, the experts with their specific knowledge can shape the course of political debate, public policy, and indeed, shape the truth. Again, reflect on the medicalization of our lives, our children.

Foucault emphasized the essential political problem for the intellectual is not to criticize the ideological contents supposedly linked to science, or to ensure that his own scientific practice is accompanied by a correct ideology, but that of ascertaining the possibility of constituting a new politics of truth, a new class of conversation. The problem is not changing people's consciousness, or what's in their heads, but the political, economic, institutional regime of the production of the truth, the nature of the discourse. Thus we must change what is discussed and open new spaces.

On his way back from Paris, Gullivan reflected on his intense encounter with Foucault. So, power pervades all human relations, it is omnipresent, it is coterminous with condition of social relations in general. It facilitates the discourse, the generation of the truth, leads to agreement and action, it creates the condition of possibilities which are only finitely modifiable at any given time and place. With this perspective one can possibly explain what could and could not happen in Macromol, say from the late 80's to late 90's. Also, it seems that one should look at strategy as the opportunity that the current discourses, programs, technologies (human) create by chance. Strategy defined as a specific mechanism, a method to get what you want should also be examined in the light of what opportunities such a course of action, or generation of new semantic spaces may provide. If we learn how to discuss "such," we can perhaps sequentially learn to act on "such and such."

From Foucault to the Ideas in Good Currency About Leadership

Those that have the gold, have the power.
A person who doesn't know but knows that he doesn't know is a student; teach him.
A person who knows but who doesn't know that he knows is asleep; awaken him.
But a person who knows and knows that he knows is wise; follow him. – Old Asian Proverb

Back in Macromol, Gullivan thought about leadership, an idea very prominent in today's discourse. It seemed to him that the concept of leadership has changed markedly over the past few decades. Several decades ago, the concept of leadership mostly referred to the political or military domain. There was the leader of the party, the leader of the expedition or the leader, the general in battle. So in the sense of Foucault, how did the concept of leadership come to have its present meaning? Again, in the sense of Foucault, who did or does the discourse about leadership serve?

Gullivan said that, indeed, our current understanding of leadership differs substantively from the recent past, and we need to reflect on why this is so. But, first he said, let's look at leadership, the leader, the idea itself. In his world, leadership is not a property of a person, it is not primarily about personal wisdom, charisma, the will to power, and it is contingent.

It is a condition that arises in a given episteme, it is a property of a system, a description of a system, an observation by an observer. It arises when a group of people feel that their self-interest is best served when individuals or perhaps a group of individuals, are selected to represent them. They, the followers, give their trust, loyalty and their resources, in their own interest to get what they want. Without the leader/follower relationship, or structure, the followers, or indeed, the leader, could not get what they wanted. The primary benefit of this structure is clarity and assumed validity of purpose. This clarity and validity of purpose allow for coordinated action in the pursuit of goals. The constraints of the structure or relationship create freedom, and the will to act. As Fromm noted, freedom is created by boundaries, which you would know if you play any sport, say tennis. Leadership arises naturally in all social systems, be they primates or Homo sapiens sapiens. Some individuals such as the alpha male appear to have a greater biological predisposition to assume the leadership position than others in the social system.

However, language, in its capacity to create the prevailing truth, plays a central role in leadership in human social systems, and again, we might ask, whom does the discourse serve? If we look back in history at a leader such as Napoleon, we note from his writings that, along with his personal ambitions and will to power, he spent a great deal of time and attention reading the lives of other great leaders, such as Alexander the Great, Caesar, Hannibal, and he noted that they all paid a great deal of attention to detail, all manner of detail about warfare, tactics and strategy, the condition and preparedness of the troops, the distinctive role of officers, commanders, generals and the politicians of their time. They were, in Napoleon's view, masters of administration, and indeed, their successes arose from this dedication to detail and their willingness to move fast and to "take chances." These notions of the leader/administrator lasted until the middle of the last century. So what changed?

Gullivan believed that the general episteme began to change with the increasing acceptance of the economic doctrine of Hayek, the doctrine of laisse faire, that government interference leads to socialism, which is antithetical to freedom and democracy. Friedrich A. Hayek got the Nobel Prize in Economics in 1974 and his views were similar to those of Milton Friedman and the "Chicago School." With the increasing acceptance of this "truth" in the Anglo-Saxon world and, to some extent the world of Adam Smith, the idea of deregulation began to take hold in the mid-to-late-70's; a small idea can often have great consequences, again as Tolstoy noted. If we look at the geometric growth in the replication of ideas and the legitimacy of deregulation, we can note the concomitant geometric growth in the rise of the share of surplus accrued by the Princes themselves and the decline in the idea of the welfare state and the rapid rise in the GINI index which measures the national distribution of income. The relative share of the income taken by the Princes has risen over the past few decades from about 20/30 times that of the average worker to now over 500 times that of the average worker. Against this perspective, it was clearly in the interest of the business/academic authors to extol the virtues of leadership, to ascribe the business success to the personage of the leader. They, the academic institutions, received much funding and status in return, from these leaders they chose to extol. The professors were indeed in good company.

The number of books with the word "leadership" in their titles rose exponentially from about 5 to 10 in the mid-70's to about 500+ today. Today there are whole sections in the library on leadership, there are thousands of courses, seminars, workshops on leadership at all levels of an organization. There are, indeed, now many institutes on leadership, where many experts make a good living. After all, says the Prince, if I am a leader and no longer just an administrator, I deserve my larger and ever larger share of the surplus, so the discourse on leadership, the new "truth" of leadership, serves the Princes and the academic institutions. So Gullivan said I am aware that this is a politically sensitive issue, but why should this not be of concern?

Gullivan said, remember the words of Walt Whitman, "to the extent we have heroes, we diminish ourselves." Gullivan remembered when Macromol was in its golden age. In that time, the number of options, possibilities for good investment making, arising from the core of Macromol, exceeded the resources available in Macromol to take full advantage of them. As Macromol devolved and the space of possibilities contracted in the sense of what could be discussed, the direction of the flow of possibilities reversed. The "strategy" came increasingly from the top down. This is, indeed, one of the key symptoms of a devolving organization. If we go back to Ashby and his law of requisite variety (for appropriate regulation), the variety in the regulator must be equal to or greater than the variety in the system being regulated. In other words, a system can only model (discuss) something to the extent that it has sufficient internal variety to represent (discuss) it. Thus, the variety of options, spaces or domain of future possibilities, open to and discussable by the population of Macromol, with the variety of interests and connections to the world at large, will always be greater than the conservative subsystem of the Prince and his Cardinals. When the number, variety and intensity of the directives flowing from the top down exceed those coming from the "core" up, the system will, by natural selection, devolve. The rituals of leadership groups, i.e. no longer self-viewed as administrators, will by virtue of their self-defined exclusivity, limit the variety that can be discussed, hence, agreed upon and, consequently, acted upon. So the prevailing idea of leadership can, indeed have unwanted consequences. Gullivan noted that there also seemed to be a coterminous exponential growth in management theories, and Gullivan asked, how and why did this happen?

Gullivan replied that once again, we should revisit the insights of Foucault. As Foucault noted, strategy lies at the intersection between the discourses, the programs, and the technology. Now if we reflect on the discourses and programs of deregulation, and the rise of the technology of human resources, we can see where the contingent space of possibility for the management gurus to arise, replicate and proliferate. If one goes back to the just prior time, there were just a handful of gurus whose books were widely read, such as Peter Drucker, Max Weber, Herbert Simon, Alfred Chandler and Joseph Schumpeter. These authors wrote mostly in an intellectual and descriptive mode, describing the history and prehistory of the day. They did not proceed to preach what policies should be adopted, but perhaps regarded their work as policy inputs. The role of the author, management guru, began to change.

They began to give advice, many began to write about success stories and concluded that if others would just follow their conclusions, their advice, they, too, would be successful. This opportunistic snapshot view of the successful with their superficial analysis, of course, led many to follow the "wrong" path. Just as with books on leadership, we now have libraries of how-to books and legions of those endeavoring to make a living in the business of giving expert advice. The latest fads, whether it be reengineering, quality or empowerment, receive wide acclaim, become the discourse in good currency, and of course, perhaps as a relief, divert the discourse from the business of business. Indeed, in order to give these academic practitioners the cloak of respectability, administration was now called management science.

This cloak, in Gullivan's opinion, led many further astray, since the language of biology of self-interest is far more powerful than the language of science in this problem space (business). To highlight the slippery ground on which these fads are anchored, let me by way of example refer to one of my favorite management intellectuals, Donald Schön. Gullivan spent many hours talking to Don about "management" issues, and he remembered well Don's remarks that the only value management added was to allay the anxiety of the managed. Gullivan would expand on this and say if the management provides clarity and validity of purpose, the group can devote their scarce resources of time, energy and attention to the mutually agreed upon tasks as opposed to dissipating their energies internally in anxiety.

Don Schön and Chris Argyris in their book, *Organizational Learning, A Theory of Action Perspective*, asked the question, "What is an organization that it can learn?" Their choice of language is noteworthy and, in Gullivan's view, predictive of the class of possible answers. They wrote, "an organization *is* a government, or polis, an agency, a task system, a theory of action, a cognitive enterprise undertaken by individual members, a cognitive artifact made up of individual images and public maps." (Emphasis theirs.) They proceed to define and discuss single loop learning, or how the "members" of the organization respond to changes in the internal and external environments of the organization by detecting and correcting errors which they then correct so as to maintain the central features of the organizational theory in use. They then proceed to define and discuss double-loop learning – the name "double loop" refers to those sorts of organizational inquiry which resolve incompatible organizational rules by setting new priorities and weightings of rules, or by restructuring the rules themselves together with associated strategies and assumptions. They discuss what is discussable, what is not discussable, and distinguish between the espoused theory and the theory in use.

Both of these authors and Stafford Beer have added greatly to our under-standing of business social systems, Gullivan noted. However, suppose they started from a more biologically embodied perspective. Gullivan said he believed that they would have taken a different path. Suppose they started, as Gullivan did, from the description of an organization, or indeed, any system as a set of communicating parts, a human organization or system as a set of agreements in language, such that the "agreers" get what they want. Suppose they used Ashby's explanation of learning and adapting, and Foucault's understanding of the nature of power, truth, what discourses are permissible and Maturana's explanations on what is conserved, and what, therefore, is the domain of possible change. It is not surprising that Schön/Argyris, as they stated in their book, never saw a real case of double-loop learning, i.e., a change of mind set, a change in the strategic conversation, or most importantly, a change in the fundamental mode of productivity, a change in the truth.

Gullivan believed that double-loop learning is well-nigh impossible under typical circumstances. Consider that it is in the self-interest of the current "executive structure" to conserve their manner of living, their strategic conversation, their truth, its history and its projection into the future. To bring about double-loop learning, transformation, regenerative change, it is by definition necessary to change the strategic conversation which in turn requires the acceptance of a new "truth" which in itself requires a new language. Now we all know that there is a high bio-cost, time, energy, attention, desire, required to learn a new language, a subject Gullivan said he would expand on shortly. For a group to do so presents a bio-cost problem of 2n class (2 to the power of n, the number in the group). "Successful" people do not seek to change their mindsets. Now we all know that it is politically desirable to be heard talking about fundamental change, transformation, but it does not reach the field of action. The wanting is not there, the language is not there, its absence is not recognized, and the personal cost is too high, impossibly high. So then what are the conditions of possibility such that a business social system can transform, or more appropriately, regenerate itself?

BOOK IV

BEGINNING TO UNCOVER THE "RULES" FOR REGENERATIVE CHANGE BY DESIGN

The Creative Conservation of Capital

More important than learning how to recall things is finding ways to forget things that are cluttering the mind. – Eric Butterworth

All learning requires trial and error, even if this trial and error process is in the mind's eye. All investments are preceded by agreements, which are preceded by discourse. For regenerative change, the discourse must change, the truth, the language must change. Change in language, except in unusual circumstances, involves new knowers. The language the new knower speaks is the language of the new mode of productivity in the "domain of business." The appropriate discourse must be such that it is possible in principle, having the requisite variety of knowers to fashion an agreement, and investment where the primary mode of productivity is based on the new abundant resource. This is distinctly different than improving the industrial business model through the incorporation of the new tools.

The mode of productivity of the "Old Economy," the Industrial Age (up to 1970), was based on the reduction in the cost of a unit of work (at a time of cheap energy). This is simply an amplification of the muscles. This was discussable, thinkable, and all the cogent actions of the corporation reflected this truth; the business plan, investments, and market strategies. However, there has been a major shift, noticed but not yet explained by economists (perhaps economics should be left to the biologists, not disembodied mathematics), because the mode of productivity of the "New Economy" is based on the reduction in the cost of reducing uncertainty. This is simply an amplification of the nervous system. The existence of confusion over the relationship of productivity and employment in the early phases of the new economy – if productivity is going up, why is employment also going up? – can be explained by saying that the new concept of productivity is not discussable in the old language (output of stuff per man hour), and so cannot be appropriately reflected in the business plan, investments, and market strategies of most old corporations.

Now, to restate, let's look at the social system of management theorists and at their disembodied perspective on change, for example, from the perspective of Schön and Argyris. Single-loop learning: detect and correct errors, as confined by the existing belief system, in order to dynamically stay essentially the same. For example, "productivity depends on lower-cost work, so we must invest in more efficient machines." Double-loop learning: detect and correct errors in the belief system itself. The process requires the development, of a new set of social essential variables, which means a change in the business theory – a change in "the truth" – and a change in the interpretation of "productivity now," to lowering the cost of reducing uncertainty and its economic significance.

Is it any wonder that Schön and Argyris never observed double-loop learning, as noted above? The inherent resistance to change of belief systems, including the vast bio-cost, means that it is nearly impossible for an existing organization to come to a new belief system on its own, without the intervention of a specific process that is designed to bring it about without destroying the existing system. The individuals – whether deep in the hierarchy or in the court – are too vulnerable, and their need to be secure and know that they can make a living and survive in the social order of the existing organization is too great for all to be comfortable in the face of the necessary change. They may know intuitively that change is needed, but do not have the requisite variety in language to know how to discuss a secure path forward.

Gullivan said that we can apply this reasoning to management theorists in turn. Though Schön and Argyris referenced Ashby, could they, with their background and focus, have seen the deep implications of Ashby's work? Why did they not follow the reasoning from Ashby into social systems? Gullivan's hypothesis is that, because they were not structurally coupled to a business, it was impossible for these professors, as smart as they were, to see what can only be seen by direct experience of the social system of the corporation. Talking about double-loop learning is a comfortable way to make a living, but double-loop learning does not happen in the field of action. Coming to a new understanding is hard.

Consider the bio-cost to a single individual to learn a new language, change an entire belief system, change what is considered the truth, change the manner of making a living – all factors which are conserved. Now think of such a change at the social level, which is on the order of a 2n-type problem (2 to the power of group size) because the system is relational – each subsystem has to interact with all others, and each subsystem has internal relations of the same order. Consider these circumstances and reflect on the total bio-cost – time, energy, attention, stress – to change what is in place, while staying alive.

The Bio-Cost of Learning

The things we know best are the things we haven't been taught. – Vauvenargues

Then Gullivan began to discuss the cost involved in learning. Trial-and-error learning has a "bio-cost," a construct for the measurable, biological cost to any system performing an activity in pursuit of "getting what it wants." Gullivan said, "I define the elements of bio-cost to be the drawdown on resources available to the system: time, energy, and attention. In addition, the demands on resources lead to an additional component, that of stress, which is a complicating factor in systems that include a hormone system cross-tabbed to the nervous system."

In the context of bio-cost, let's review the complex task that Ashby proposed in *Design for a Brain*, the task of wanting a set of 1,000 spinning wheels to all be stopped in the same position, with the letter "A" facing up. There are three cases to consider:

- **Case 1** construes the task as completely parallel in nature, starting by spinning all the wheels at once. The likelihood that all the wheels will end up in the correct position is 2 to the power of the number of wheels, or nothing short of astronomical. Waiting for this probability to payoff is clearly futile.

- **Case 2** takes the opposite tack, executing the task completely serially, and one wheel at a time until the spin is correct. Each subsystem is taken independently of each other, and each is worked on until correct. The time taken is tractable.

- **Case 3** is a mixed approach, where every subsystem is started and failures are restarted until all are correct. Clearly this takes more than 1 spin, but less than Case 2 because many subsystems are working in parallel.

What are the lessons from this simple exemplar of complex tasks? Changing everything at once and hoping that it will all fall into place is futile, as seen in the vast average time taken in Case 1. Experience shows this approach is very common, even though it does not take advantage of intermediate, partial results. A complex task can only be accomplished if broken down into independent subsystems. We can do that breakdown in a couple of ways. In Case 3, we try everything at once. Many subsystems are in play at the same time and it appears to have low total bio-cost. But there is a huge disturbance internal to the system, with so many subsystems in motion simultaneously. This requires attention distributed across too many different contexts, with high demands for communication across subsystems, leading to confusion and potentially paralysis and death. In Ashby's terms, the demand on the "channel capacity" is too high. Complex environments must be approached part-by-part with little or no communication between the parts until assembly when each subsystem comes together and is integrated into the whole. This is Case 2. Each subsystem can learn on its own, sequentially, and then all the subsystems can be integrated into a whole.

We see from this example what we know from experience: that learning to accomplish complex tasks is hard work and involves high bio-cost. Environmental disturbance, resulting in disturbances to the essential variables, is also costly. To limit disturbances, every system "simplifies complexity." The entire construct of the "scientific laboratory" provides buffers – we don't see and we don't hear a huge range of complexity in order to deal with simplifications – so that we can learn about the world in parts, sequentially (otherwise we can't do science). Because of our fragile biology, discussed earlier, we build "stabilizers" that enable us to more easily maintain the essential variables of biological life, such as houses with roofs and insulation and heating systems. In daily life, habits are simplifications that shield us from too much complexity, only one of countless examples of cognitive responses to the high bio-cost of living.

To repeat, Gullivan said systems avoid or dismiss complexity because it is too costly to engage it, and it might even kill them. To survive as the environment changes, systems must learn, but learning is costly. A given system has limits as to the environment to which it can adapt. It may not have the requisite variety or the capacity to learn fast enough. As observers we can note the significant, natural resistance to learning to adapt to complex environment – the bio-cost is high, and the benefits are almost certainly unclear to the beneficiaries. It is possible to amplify learning in an existing system – a child can be taught new words, or can be given a dictionary and "exceed" the system's requisite variety, as noted earlier. Systems can successfully expand their variety if they learn part-by-part, serially; maintain clarity in the local subsystem they are engaged in while learning; and avoid over communication between subsystems; indeed, as in speciation, a physical separation of subsystems, is usually necessary. Einstein made the most of his contribution when he was isolated from the academic physics community. The forces that maintain the status quo in the social system are huge. Here are three possible ways to bring about regenerative change in the face of them:

1. **Machiavelli:** We kill the Prince and all those around him that speak the truth as he does. The new Prince brings with him the new truth. This, for example, is what happened on an island where computers were made in the 1990's when a new Prince made huge changes at great social cost – the sale of social assets in the form of layoffs for thousands of employees, including those that spoke the old truth.

2. **Philosopher Prince:** There may exist a Prince who has a dream and owns the truth, and who can move the entire strategic discussion from his existing position. The approach is to allow the

old and still to build the new. As unlikely as this sounds, it does happen, as for example, an island historically spoke the language of wood, rubber, manufacturing electrical cables. Yet the Prince, on his own, began to include discourses about cell phones and social communication, and thereby a new business was conceived. A new truth, a separate new social system, was created, the child was supported by the parent, the surpluses from the old school.

3. **By Design:** Gullivan said, based on the understanding outlined above, working from Ashby through to Foucault and Maturana, that it is possible in principle to bring about regenerative change in an existing organization, including a change in the mode of productivity from mass/energy solutions to information solutions – as Gullivan put it earlier, from reduction in the unit-cost of work, to reduction in the unit-cost of reducing uncertainty. Gullivan said that he did not know that this has ever been done, and has shown the reasons why it is so unlikely. R&D is subject to the existing Prince and is limited by the language of the Prince. The Prince is constrained by his need to portray a bright future right now. He lives in the land of efficiencies and urgency of today, where he defines his self-interest and his history and the history of the Organization. If the Prince does not know that he does not know, then he thinks he knows.

The Creative Conservation of Capital

Pour new wine into new wineskins. – Zen Saying

On a very pleasant afternoon a few summers after Gullivan left the island of Macromol, he sat in his garden under the old walnut tree and reflected on his three-decade journey through time in Macromol, his experiences, his journey as the Jester in court, his journey to meet with the sages to find answers to his puzzles. How could he recognize a good investment? One where the surplus created could be reinvested in the same business space to yield an even greater surplus. Why did the members of the court continue in non-generative investments?

His thoughts turned to the concept of the "creative destruction of capital" as put forward by Schumpeter, and natural selection or, indeed, elimination as invented by Darwin. The creative destruction of capital seems to be how the world works, the nature of things, but is this destruction of capital really necessary, at least at the level of social capital? Gullivan noted the population in Macromol had decreased over the years to a point that it was barely half the size of that it was when he first arrived in Macromol. Is it not possible, Gullivan thought, to specify conditions such that we can have the creative conservation of social capital? Yes, indeed, it is possible to specify such conditions but to create such conditions requires a radical change, in Schön's words, a change in the theory in use.

If we look at living systems as strategies for making a living, those strategies that fail to reproduce fast enough in a given ecosystem and at a given time are eliminated. Natural elimination selects against the rate of reproduction, generativity. To understand natural elimination and what replications are eliminated, said Gullivan, let's go back in time.

Lamarck, several decades before Darwin, postulated that evolution occurred through the passing on from generation to generation, of characteristics acquired during the life of the "individual." For example, as the giraffe stretched its neck further and further to reach the leaves on the tall trees, its neck grew longer and longer and this long neck was passed on to its offspring, who in turn continued the process of neck stretching. As later biologists would show, Lamarck may not be entirely wrong. Darwin invented the concept of natural selection where evolution favors those strategies or learning entities that reproduce, or replicate fastest, inasmuch as all living systems in an ecosystem compete for resources. Darwin opened up a new semantic space with all its possibilities. Darwin inferred from his many and detailed observations that natural selection was, indeed, the mechanism of evolution.

While Darwin was on his journeys, an Austrian monk, away from the everyday world in the monastery, was busy at work cross-breeding many varieties of peas. The monk, Mendel, was a brilliant experimenter and mathematician, and using the abstract language of mathematics to make sense out of what he observed, he concluded that the germ cells, say the egg and the sperm cells, had half as much heritable information as that contained in the body cells, and that as the germ cells were formed, there was some kind of reductive division. Thus, Mendel opened up a new semantic space – genetics – even though he could not see the genes or the chromosomes at that time.

What Gullivan found interesting was that Darwin, though puzzled as to how in detail natural selection worked, he could not think about genes, he could not discuss the subject, he did not know that he did not know. At the turn of the 20th century when Mendel's work was rediscovered, the biologists began to put Mendel's and Darwin's (and Wallace's) ideas together. Through many experiments, publication, conversations, the biologists arrived at a grand synthesis called the Central Dogma, which claimed that the gene was the result of heredity, the DNA sequence, and heredity became associated with DNA replication. Changes or mutations in the gene or DNA could be passed on but no characteristic acquired by the body could be inherited. Then Watson and Crick elucidated the structure of DNA, and they opened up the semantic space of modern molecular biology.

But, of course, the DNA has no meaning, in the living sense, considered by itself. The gene uses the apparatus of the cells, the egg and the sperm cell, to replicate itself and thus pass on information. The unit of the living is not DNA or the gene, part of the DNA sequence, but the cell. The question is, is the cell silent in passing on information or instructions? Modern biologists think not, perhaps there is a possibility of Lamarckianism at the level above the gene, the chemistry at the proximate level, the sheath surrounding the gene, the level of the body, say the placenta, and perhaps the multibody or the social level, i.e., above the gene or what is now called the epigenetic level. At the epigenetic level, what variations in what replicators are present and available to the process of natural elimination or selection? Of course, for us humans, this leads us to the domain of language, and the possibility, and indeed, probability that at the epigenetic level the cell "memory" can be passed on to future generations. While the DNA itself is not affected by the history of the individual, the "behavior" of the gene, whether it is switched on or off, or indeed, fully on or off, may well be affected. Does our thinking affect the degree to which the gene is on or off, and hence the amount of protein that gene codes for, a whole new semantic space with all its possibilities?

Dawkins invented the concept of the meme, a unit of information for the nervous system with a replicator, a form of language, or symbol, which could be subject at the epigenetic or social level to natural selection. Gullivan preferred to cast the meme as a piece of conversation or communication, that pattern of memes that make up conversations in particular domains such as biology, physics, electronics, or nanotechnology. Although the conversations the biologists have today are very different than those that Mendel, Lamarck, Darwin or Wallace had in their time, today's biologist can trace back the lineage of their conversations to the earlier biologists.

If we return to Macromol and consider Ashby's concepts, modified to fit social systems and focus on the social essential variables, we can see that variety of possible parameters, which in action can be seen as conversations or strategies for making a living, determines the capacity of the social system in Macromol to adapt to changes in the environment, to adapt for the better, to be evolutionary current. As Maturana said, people always, from the viewpoint of a biologist, do what they want to do, so we can say that at the court there was insufficient variety in the discussions that led to agreements and investments to adapt and overcome the need for half the population to leave Macromol, and find other ways and other places in which to make a living. So in order to have the capacity to adapt to the changing environment, the court must have at least the requisite variety of strategies available to it to continue to be fully adapted to the environment at large. In the context of improving efficiency, the language narrows, narrows in the Blue Phase, such that the variety of strategies available for selection decreases, the domain of reason narrows and those potential new strategies or conversations seen as reasonable outside Macromol are viewed as "unreason" inside Macromol.

We may look at a new class of strategies or conversations and ask the question, how does this new class come about such that it may be selected to adapt for the better? A new class of conversation is analogous to a new species in the domain of language, so how do new species arise, what Darwin called the mystery of mysteries? Today most biologists agree on an explanation akin to the following: Supposing in a fertile valley there was a large herd of deer, thriving, feeding on many of the plants in the valley, from generation to generation, they were fully adapted to their ecosystem. Being fully adapted and content, their genetic variety was relatively low, they were efficient. Indeed, they were so efficient that the valley became overpopulated. Sensing the overcrowding, a small group left the valley slowly making their way westward until after many generations they settled in a new valley quite different than the valley in which their ancestors now continue to live. The genetic variety in the small isolated group was now subject to new selection pressures. We know that mutations to the genes can and do occur, but rarely do such mutations confer survival benefits. However, there are many degrees of variation in the genes brought about via sexual reproduction. First, there is the mixing of genes from the male and female. Before that when a body cell divided to form a germ cell with half the amount of genetic information, that half, if say the deer had 20 chromosomes (DNA and its packaging), 20 long strings of information, and the number of possible combinations is in the millions. Additionally during germ cell formation, the information strings, the chromosomes pair up and exchange bits of information giving rise to another very high degree of potential variation. Now over time, the selection pressures in the new ecosystem selected out those variants that did not fit the new realty, left in those variants that conferred survival benefits, such that the new west deer could no longer interbreed, were they by chance to meet, with the deer now in the original valley. Successful speciation required *stress that led to migration, isolation and sufficient genetic variety, the requisite variety from which to select to become adapted to the new environment.* The two herds of deer could no longer interbreed because the languages of their genetic codes were no longer compatible, they could no longer map one language onto the other.

In Macromol, as it enters the Blue Phase, the variety of potential strategies from which to select, to adapt to the changing environment outside Macromol decreases. To the extent that the Prince controls, and sends instructions down, the variety in Macromol is correspondingly further attenuated. Meanwhile, variety with the changing mode of productivity in the larger environment, is increasing. As Ashby noted in his "Law of Requisite Variety," it takes increasing variety in the controller to regulate increasing variety in the controlled, or the environment.

So how can variety be increased by design in Macromol?

Enter the Queen: The Designer

You can only find truth with logic if you have already found truth without it. – G. K. Chesterton

Assuming, said Gullivan, that killing the Prince and changing the truth, and the improbable event that a new philosopher Prince will arrive in Macromol, what must occur such that regenerative change can take place in Macromol, such that a new Red Phase is born? Gullivan said that a certain kind of person is required to bring about such an event, this person I call the Queen, the mother of a new species.

The role of increasing variety falls to the "Queen," a concept which Gullivan will elaborate on later. Although the Prince, through the drive for efficiency, brought about a decrease in variety consistent with maturity in the Blue Phase, this decrease is not necessarily a problem as long as a Queen and resources from the surpluses derived in the Blue Phase are present, and the Queen has developed the appropriate increase in variety. Now to do this, the Queen must be isolated. The Queen and those in the "nursery," the new businesses that are evolutionary, current speak a different language than the Prince and one cannot map the old Blue language onto the new Red language – they are different species of languages. Now how could the Queen have increased the variety in Macromol if she had the required resources and was isolated? Assuming that the Queen was fully functional, what did she do?

Imagine the story if a Queen in the late Green or early Blue Phase left the Island of Macromol in search of new variety. She knew that the new variety could be found in the new semantic spaces opened up by the inventors, the space of potential discoveries. These spaces as noted earlier were in the domains of information technology, biotechnology, nanotechnology and new classes of materials. Fully understanding the power of these technologies to create order out of disorder, relative certainty out of uncertainty, she was able to select focusing problems in these new domains. The focusing problems were members of a class of problems in each domain such that their solutions could be replicated in and perhaps across domains, i.e., their solutions were generative, the surpluses generated in practice could be reinvested to create even greater surpluses. The Queen fully understood the economic potential inherent in each class of problems, and was aware of the critical importance of picking the appropriate focusing problem. She was careful to remain in isolation and not to try to solve the problems in the mature Blue Phase, not to replace the products in the Blue Phase with similar products using the new technologies. Such a course she knew would forestall speciation, a step change and drastically limit the potential new variety in Macromol. A previous Queen had done the above in the very early stages of the Red Phase in Macromol. She had brought to Macromol a scientist who knew the language of macromolecules and asked him to solve the problem of making strong string out of such molecules.

Then Gullivan remembered how unusual, how rigorous and how difficult the process of recognizing the latent power inherent in new semantic spaces is, how difficult it is to pick the right focusing problem, and how difficult it is in practice to retain the autonomy and isolation necessary for successful birth, speciation and development. If the Queen had been fully functioning and successful in her isolation, perhaps the population in Macromol would still be as evolutionarily current as it was when Gullivan first entered the island.

Unlike the Prince, the Queen lives in the land of new semantic spaces. She is well aware of the new insights, intuitions and discovery spaces being opened. She is aware of their potential and can speak the new language. The new semantic spaces arise as mutations in the truth. These mutations arise in the mind of the intuitive. As Einstein said, "I do not think in language, I think in images." The intuitors are rare, perhaps one in a million or perhaps one in ten or a hundred million, rare like successful mutations in biology. Characteristically, the intuitors are possessed by a problem in theory: the meaning-making system itself. They have the capacity to concentrate, to accept the relative social isolation, and the problem of being misunderstood. Many in history were described as preoccupied, absent minded, or a little odd. Through concentration and frustration they break through to the new truth. The intuitive process is not in the domain of everyday language, analysis or logic, it is in the domain of direct knowing, and indeed, is essentially the same as that used by the Zen Master. Having "seen" the new truth through direct knowing, the problem arises (if they so choose) for the intuitor, how shall he communicate the new truth?

Einstein spent a great deal of time thinking about thinking, and has much to say on the subject and about the intuitive process in particular. He wrote in his *Autobiographical Notes* (1946): "There is no inductive method which could lead to the fundamental concepts of physics. Failure to understand this fact constituted the basic philosophical error of so many investigators of the nineteenth century."

He added, what, precisely, is "thinking"? When, at the reception of sense-impressions, memory-pictures emerge, this is not yet "thinking." And when such pictures form series, each member of which calls forth another, this too, is not yet "thinking." When, however, a certain picture turns up in many such series, then – precisely through such return – it becomes an *ordering element* for such series, in that it *connects series* which in themselves are unconnected. Such an element becomes an instrument, a *concept*. I think that the transition from free association of "dreaming" to thinking is characterized by the more or less dominating role which the "concept" plays in it. It is by no means necessary that a concept must be connected with a sensorially-cognizable and reproducible *sign* (word); but when this is the case, thinking becomes, by means of that fact, *communicable*.

In 1905 Einstein published his rather unusual type of scientific paper (i.e., not the usual introduction, data and analysis and conclusions) on special relativity. It took the scientific elite almost 5 years to realize what he was saying: it was not an improvement on the electrodynamics of Lorentz and Maxwell, but was, indeed, a radical change in the meaning of time itself, as noted earlier. Indeed, it sometimes takes generations to appreciate radical change in the truth, e.g., Mendel's studies on genetics, or Wegener's and later Holmes' theories on tectonic plates and continental drift.

It should be noted that Einstein's contemporaries did not really see any problem with time as an invariant. However, the intuitive Einstein was bothered with the prevailing truth for over ten years. It should also be noted that he arrived at these insights when he was safely outside the system and politics of science, working as a patent clerk, which gave him ample "space" to pursue his intuitions. As he noted in his commemorative publication in honor of the 80th birthday of Leo Baeck in 1953, "Few people are capable of expressing with equanimity opinions which differ from the prejudices of their social environment. Most people are incapable of forming such opinions."

So how can a social system change by design? What are the necessary and sufficient conditions such that regeneration is possible?

Now the Queen has special talents – she can understand the nature of opening a new space, a new truth. The Queen is able to recognize and select from those new spaces the ones most relevant to the regenerative process for her social system – the island, with its history and resources. She can translate these selections into specific, relevant problems and explain aspects such as the economic potential of these new spaces, how to proceed to "take the ignorance out of it," to bring order to disorder, and to create new distinctions in language such that the new truth becomes communicable. This constitutes productive action in the second class of change, discovery, and precedes the logical continuance in the phase of efficiency. The Queen, who forms the bridge from the intuiters to birth, development and eventual embodiment in the larger social system, is a rare and special person.

The Queen cannot be subject to the Prince. They cannot even communicate in the Ashby or Pask sense. Perhaps the Prince thinks the Queen "speaks in tongues." The Queen must own the semantically isolated "nursery" in which new language is born.

So, "regenerative change by design" is simple biology – conception through mixing of existing languages to make new language, birth, development. Perhaps Gordon Pask has the best formalism to further explore the details of this developmental path, in language, of the social truth in organizations; as Schumpeter said:

> *Capitalism, then, is by nature a form or method of economic change and, not only never is, but never can be stationary. And this evolutionary character of the capitalist process is not merely due to the fact that economic life goes on in a social and natural environment which changes and by its change alters the data of economic action; this fact is important and these changes (wars, revolutions and so on) often condition industrial change, but they are not its prime movers. Nor is this evolutionary character due to a quasi-automatic increase in population and capital or to the vagaries of monetary systems of which exactly the same thing hold true. The fundamental impulse that sets and keeps the capitalist engine in motion comes from the new consumers' goods, the new methods of production or transportation, the new markets, the new forms of industrial organization that capitalist enterprise creates.*
>
> *…The opening up of new markets, foreign or domestic, and the organizational development from the craft shop and factory to such concerns at U.S. Steel illustrate the same process of industrial mutation – if I may use that biological term – that incessantly revolutionizes the economic structure from within, incessantly destroying the old one, incessantly creating a new one. This process of Creative Destruction is the essential fact about capitalism. It is what capitalism consists of and what every capitalist concern has got to live in…*

However, the destruction of social systems, the huge loss of capital and concomitant rise in misery is not necessary if we look to evolution and learn how to bring about appropriate change by design.

When to Find a Queen, and What Next?

When you can do nothing, what can you do? – Zen Koan

"I am," Gullivan said, "by nature, not a morning person and on early morning flights to Boston, I usually tend to fall half-asleep and dream." On one such flight to attend a conference on developments in electronics, he was dreaming about change and what were the conditions of possibility that must exist in order for transformational change, a change in the truth, to occur in Macromol. The world was changing and Macromol was devolving day by day; its course reminded him of Bertalanffy's notion of equifinality. He wondered whether it was even possible for any agent to bring about significant change. He thought not, but it might be possible to figure out the conditions of possibility, and then run some test or experiment to convince himself that he was on track. The "failed" experiment teaches, so if his experiment failed, perhaps he could then, through direct experience, understand why it failed, and thereby see what conditions of possibility were absent. He remembered a marketing course he took long ago on marketing failures. It impressed him that out of say ten key factors, if one was "missing," this led to failure. Studying success, on the other hand, just glorified a few factors, ignored context, and very often attributed the success to a few key individuals. Success does not teach very much, it's the errors that teach. That is why medical advances come from the study of the sick, not the healthy. So what experiment should he "set up?" Where are the Queens? If he met a Queen, how would he recognize her... perhaps a koan?

By now he had arrived at Kresge Hall, proceeded to get his badge, pick up some of the papers, got a cup of coffee, and sat down to learn about the latest in thinking about electronics. At lunch in the Student Hall, he sat beside a professor from MIT. She was tall, fit-looking, with long dark hair and deep blue-gray eyes. What drew his attention was the intensity of her gaze that promised a capacity to concentrate, a keen intellect, a sense of equanimity, yet awareness. Yes, she was awake. As he talked to her, he found that she was a professor in biology, but also had a Ph.D. in philosophy, and here she was at a forum on electronics. At first, the conversation was about data compression, how little data we really need, in as much as we fill in the rest, indeed 80% of the neuronal activity, in the usual experience of seeing is outside the light activated parts of the nervous system. He wondered if we really make up what we see.

After lunch, he made arrangements to meet the professor for dinner later on that evening. He met Catherine Jane Wainright at around 7 o'clock at the Marriott, and as they sat down for dinner at an elegant corner table, she said, "By the way, my friends call me CJ" They began to discuss the strangeness of quantum computing and the problems associated with real-time language translation. Between tasty morsels of rack of lamb, she asked him what exactly he did at Macromol, and what was his interest in electronics and computing? He replied that with the support of a select few Cardinals there, he was trying to help them bring about a rebirth in the once mighty Macromol. Although it appeared to many at Macromol that he had a lot of freedom to pursue what he thought was important, and since he did not get involved in business operations, many concluded that he did not make any visible contribution. However, under the protection of his mentors, he pursued his passion, to uncover the conditions of possibility for the rebirth of Macromol. This passion demanded that he have a good understanding of all of the major areas of technology, in particular, an understanding at the level of theory, the underlying basis for creating a new level of order out of disorder, for creating a new mode of productivity. He did not get involved in the practice, but in the question of what the practice could do, and what was the intrinsic economic potential. Being a night person he often arrived at the office at about 9 or 10 in the morning, but only a few people at Macromol realized that he very frequently worked late into the night. Since he had long since left the everyday mainstream language and ongoing business concerns at Macromol, he was understood by a small group with whom he had ongoing conversations. In the larger context at Macromol, the frequent comment was, what is he talking about, I don't understand, and what has this to do with the business, we have to stop talking and do something. Of course, the doing was just more talking, but the "conversation" was now more comfortable and rooted in the past.

CJ noted that she understood his position, somewhat, inasmuch as she often had similar experiences at MIT. Most technical communities conserve their version of the truth, and changes in the truth often meet up with considerable opposition, and often bitter personal feuds, so common in academia. How often do we hear the immediate retort, you're wrong! CJ then inquired, "What sources have you drawn on, on your journey, and where do you come out now?" He proceeded to discuss what he had learned, what he had found explanatory, useful, from the works of Pask, Maturana, Ashby, Foucault, etc. Much to his surprise and delight at the time, CJ was very familiar with Maturana's and Foucault's ideas, so they had a long conversation on how he found them useful. They were both comfortable with the idea that the truth is local and the truth is conserved and it evolves.

CJ was particularly interested in his understanding of efficiency for an economic social system, as he explained it in terms of Shannon's work on sending messages of an arbitrary level of accuracy. CJ said she never considered economic efficiency as resulting from efficiency in languaging, sending messages, encoding messages, in the historical and locally abbreviated language. As she said, this peculiar local language, its clarity by virtue of its locally common usage gave rise to economy in instructions which, in turn, was reflected in "machine" or "transaction" efficiency. Although the local language virtually eliminated misunderstanding, hence improved efficiency, it gave rise to an "evolutionary barrier," in that new, let's say, technologically and evolutionary current languaging outside Macromol, could not be expressed in the current efficient understandable language in Macromol. "These ideas explain," she said, "some of the frustration I experience in my work. If 'they' do not understand, 'they' dismiss as wrong, irrelevant, or they do not like and are 'disturbed' by these unfamiliar new ideas or distinctions."

As a biologist, CJ said all technology is an extension of our biology in the service of our own living and surviving. "So!" she said, "What are you going to do now? Clearly change by design, as you call it, must be grown; birth, morphogenesis, development, maturation, and death, and on to the next cycle. I agree with you that the key factor in changing the local truth is that someone asks the now strange question, which, in Foucault's terms, is in the domain of unreason. Since unreason is intolerable in the main body at Macromol, unreason must be allowed to occur outside the domain of reason, the new idea can only take hold in a protected zone, just as speciation requires separation from the old environment. The conversations in the protected zone will not map onto reason, i.e., the prevailing truth in Macromol. So, the Queen, as you describe it, must be autonomous, just like we try to achieve here at MIT."

CJ continued, "Suppose we know the new semantic space opened some time ago. Let's say it has evolved to the stage where at least a small community can understand the power and potential that is inherent in the new space. So, in my experience, the key to success is in picking the right problem, the 'focusing problem.' The focusing problem is necessary to bring about shared self-interest, thus create the conditions of possibility for new distinctions in language (i.e. technology) necessary for development, new instructions, and new truth."

"Yes," Gullivan said, "the focusing problem should be selected with great care; it must have, at this time in history, the following characteristics, assuming we are constraining the challenge to the domain of 'information technology'":

1. It must be of a problem class that replaces transformation of mass and energy, or uncertainty related to mass and energy, with actionable information flows – so that it participates in the new economy, takes advantage of the new abundant resource.

2. It must have economic potential – removing the uncertainty in the system/market is of high value.

3. It must be consistent with the social systems history – to connect with whom they are (their history) and what they can see themselves engaging in.

4. It must allow definition of and access to the requisite variety of domains of expertise needed to solve the problems

5. It must engage an initial set of individuals who want to do it.

6. It must serve as an exemplar or teacher for the broader social system – so that what is learned can be reproduced, and reconstructed.

By now it was well past midnight, CJ and Gullivan parted ways and agreed to meet again when he had selected a focusing problem. As he went back to his hotel, he recognized that he had acquired a new specific purpose, to select a focusing problem. He recognized that along his journey new purposes emerged, they emerged from conversation, from conversations with others and/or conversations with himself. His purpose evolved from the background.

The Experiment

Sayings remain meaningless until they are embodied in habits. – Kahlil Gibran

During the following few months, the Jester had many conversations with business leaders, technical leaders and those dealing with overall strategy in Macromol. He finally settled on a focusing problem. There was a small business, small by Macromol's standards (about $200 million) which involved producing strong string and elastic string for an article of intimate clothing which he referred to as AIC. He referred to it as AIC because the mind often wants to drift to the comfortable, concrete, and he on the other hand wanted to stay in the somewhat abstract, to permit the focus to remain on the principles, and their generality. Now, the then-current business model, or the prevailing truth, was of the classic industrial business model: guess, make stuff, store stuff, sell and deliver stuff, and guess again.

The strong and elastic strings were produced based on the best guesses of what the market needed, thus, there was a measure of uncertainty in what and when to produce. The string was modified and knitted outside Macromol, again with its uncertainty about demand. Along the chain there was a large inventory (~$2 billion) to accommodate the uncertainty of demand, the uncertainty of purchase. AIC's were made in several sizes and colors to accommodate the variety of body sizes and color preferences. Although the variety of sizes and colors was designed to cover the needs of every customer in general, it, not surprisingly, only met the needs of a few customers in particular. Again, not surprisingly, there was much dissatisfaction with individual personal fit. Personal goodness of fit is subjective inasmuch as some like their AIC's to fit tightly, others loosely, as they walk or sit, i.e., dynamic fit is subjective. Now all of these uncertainties can be eliminated or radically reduced if the right "information" or instructions are available at each appropriate point along the chain, i.e., it is a matter of computation and communication. The focusing problem then was to design a business model which used the ever-decreasing cost of reducing uncertainty as its primary mode of productivity, which would also in turn reduce not only the cost of an AIC, but the total amount of work and stored material in the entire chain to meet subjective dynamic goodness of fit for AIC's. A quick assessment at the macro level of the entire chain indicated that the production costs could, in principle, be reduced by about 30% to 40%, the large inventory of final goods could be largely eliminated and the value of the output could be increased by over 50%. The market space inherent in the new business model was at least ten times greater than that inherent in the industrial business model.

The Jester selected the focusing problem for its simplicity, its capacity to be an exemplar in Macromol and the prevailing reality that it was not in a "politically" sensitive area. If a team with the required variety of skills could transform this business, they, with the development of a new class of knower, could transform a wide range of businesses throughout Macromol. The next step was to gain the support of the Technical Courtesan who managed the allocation of resources. The Jester set about the task of acquiring the necessary resources. Richard, his friend, and the Jester had been in conversation for many years, and had a shared relevant history, so Richard clearly understood what the Jester was about. Having gotten the necessary resources to proceed, Richard and the Jester arrived at an understanding of the requisite variety of skills necessary to begin the process. They hired an outside market research group to validate the value proposition. To do this, they had AIC's made to measure, for a statistically significant number of wearers. To specify an AIC, both size and color for each wearer, they had to gather the appropriate information. This information gathering requires a conversation. Conversations have a cost, and a bio-cost, so the immediate task was how do they find the minimum set of inputs necessary to "instruct" the production system to produce the "right" AIC.

Now this process raised some interesting questions, which in turn led to some basic principles. In the past, before low cost communication and computation (uncertainty reduction), they acted as if they should first know and then act, feedback was not primary in their decision-making. However, with the ever-decreasing cost of reducing uncertainty, it is now cheaper to find out than it is to know. The task is no longer to engage in research and development in the economic system, as initiated by Edison in the past, but to design an acceptable prototype and modify it through low cost feedback, i.e. design and modify, ask, do not assume the burden of knowing. This, of course, involved the design and deployment of new infrastructure, both physical and language. Indeed, the task requires a new class of knower who shares a new truth. A second problem arose in the process which was very revealing. J.J. was one of the team members. J.J. had a background in what the Jester would call classical engineering and manufacturing and had for several years been in a group of business strategists/analysts. Although J.J. used computers daily to represent the data in more and more glorious PowerPoint charts, he had a difficult time grasping the notion of a computer as a tool to reduce uncertainty, or that there was an evolutionary and fundamental change in the mode of production in the economic system. He would often exclaim, I don't understand what you are talking about. Now this is interesting, since one cannot, in principle, decide whether the error, the misunderstanding, arises in the transmission or in the receiver. Einstein responded to this problem in saying that elegance is for carpenters and shoemakers, just keep repeating your point. Sometimes satisfactory explanations are not possible with a new truth because of the language of the speaker in trying not to be misunderstood and the codification or belief system (history) of the listener. This, once again, is why the Queen must be autonomous, she moves in a different plane.

A third point often arose which the Jester called the "pseudo-problem." For example, for Einstein once again Euclidean geometry presented a pseudo-problem in dealing with space/time. This pseudo-problem did not, however, arise when space/time was reframed in Riemannian geometry. The classical engineer, J.J., could not see how one could have a viable production system making many one-of-a-kind AIC's. This pseudo-problem disappears when one considers not a machine but a population of machines. Each machine has a programmable range of outputs. The range of sizes is finite, perhaps five or six "master" sizes and all sizes can be made with variation of these master sizes. Furthermore, many of the machines in the population are idle, so meeting the requirements of "many ones" is an informational problem. This informational problem can be handled by an information infrastructure similar to internet business today. The Jester said he could not overemphasize the significance of pseudo-problems, and its close connection to truth/power. It goes, if I don't know how to do it or understand it, how could you? You, by the way, are wrong!

After about a year's dedicated and intense work by the team, the Jester had, in essence, proof of principle – the focusing problem was on solid footing, as a business and as a powerful teacher. Along the way, however, our Courtesan mentor retired. The new Courtesan, who now controlled the resources, had no technical background and was primarily preoccupied with tomorrow's earnings or loss. A meeting with him to get the resources to launch the new business model in the market place was most illuminating. Richard and the Jester had an hour to explain the why of their project, why it was so important. During the conversation, the Jester tried to explain mutual information; it takes fewer bits of information to describe a whole system than it does to describe the parts individually because each part partly specifies the other parts. It is, like the Jester said, $(A + B)^2$ equals $A^2 + B^2 + 2AB$. I wanted to focus on the 2AB (mutual information). The Courtesan pointed out he had his under-graduate degree in mathematics and was disturbed by the position of the 2AB, as the equation is usually written $A^2 + 2AB + B^2$. He really was interested in the current problems in another business area. He "heard" what Richard and the Jester were saying, but he had no history of understanding what they were talking about, so in an hour they were dismissed. He probably could not see how he could explain this unreason to his fellow Courtesans or Cardinals. The experiment succeeded in making it clear, at least to the Jester, that the Queen must be autonomous. It is unreasonable to believe that the administrator can understand the language of the Queen, or indeed, would have any interest in such understanding. Such an understanding would involve a high bio-cost, anxiety, a fundamental change in perspective with its attendant discomfort.

It is interesting to note that practically all of the resources devoted to the focusing problem were used in conversation, meaning making, only a small part was used in making things. In the real time consumer centric model, the system is activated at the market level in real time and uses the ever-decreasing cost of reducing uncertainty as its primary mode of productivity. Although development in the domain of the above focusing problem came to an end, Gullivan knew that it was quite possible in principle to give rise to a Red Phase and that activities like those in the consumer control and consumer activated model above would occur someplace, but outside the island of Macromol. Then Richard said to the Jester, let's have a dinner party with the teachers, reflect on our journey, and discuss the Queen. The inventor or intuitor happens by chance, but one can institutionalize the concept of the Queen.

Celebrate the Journey

Wisdom is not communicable. The wisdom which a wise man tries to communicate always sounds foolish. – Hermann Hesse

Gullivan liked to cook, so he got out his favorite cookbooks and began to plan the dinner party. A first course of Irish salmon on Irish soda bread fried in butter. This would be followed by his favorite soup, homemade lobster bisque with a touch of sherry. For the main course, he selected duck, prepared by first rendering off the excess fat at high temperature in a Dutch oven, then breaking the duck into leg and breast parts, placing them on a bed of carrots, onions and white turnips in a large shallow dish, adding the seasonings and dry vermouth, covering the dish with foil and cooking for about an hour at a moderate temperature. Following that, the foil was removed and the duck broiled to the desired crisp level.

Gullivan laid out the large table in the 200-year-old dining room with a dark beamed ceiling. He selected Montrachet and Léoville Las Cases from his cellar to complement the meal.

Richard, Frank and Paul were first to arrive, followed shortly thereafter by the teachers, Erwin Schrödinger, Gordon Pask, Humberto Maturana, Gregory

Bateson, Michel Foucault, Claude Shannon, Ross Ashby, and finally Shunryu Suzuki, the Zen master. Gullivan looked around the table and reflected on who his guests were as they drank champagne and began the dinner.

Erwin Schrödinger sat to the left of Gullivan. Erwin was a tall, bushy-haired Austrian with his usual bow tie, lean frame and a smile that belied his keen intellect and extraordinary range of interests, from physics to biology and the philosophies of Schopenhauer and Spinoza. One could not fail to be struck by his presence, his intense yet engaging manner. Yes, one got the feeling that Erwin probed more deeply into life's questions than most of us.

Next to Erwin sat Gordon – Gordon Pask, the inimitable performer with cloak and umbrella. Gordon, a true Brit, was rather short and dark, but exuded a kind of whimsy, as if, between moments of seriousness, he was just about to break out in laughter or walk around as if he were on stage. Gordon was a master at the art of conversation. In fact, it was Gordon who, among his many accomplishments, developed "conversation theory," and who completely changed Gullivan's views about human conversation.

Continuing around the table, next came Humberto Maturana, with his bushy hair and very noticeable spectacles. Again one had the feeling of being in the presence of an intense intellect with a keen understanding of life. It was obvious that he was glad to be at the table with old friends. Like Erwin, Humberto was intrigued by the question, "what is life," but unlike the Austrian physicist, Humberto was a Chilean biologist. His answer was that life is a self-making autopoietic system – autonomous and structurally closed. This understanding has had a profound effect on modern philosophical discussions.

Gregory Bateson was a big man with rather round features and a shock of gray running through his swept back hair, who clearly filled the chair he was occupying. He also had the keen eyes and grin that one associates with intellectuals who enjoy the world of the mind. Gregory was originally educated as an anthropologist in England, but moved to San Francisco where he seemed very much at home. His interests ranged far and wide, but he is perhaps best known for his work in cybernetics, systems theory, psychotherapy, and human communication. Of course, he was delighted to be at the table with his old friends Gordon and Humberto.

Michel Foucault, the French philosopher, sat next to Gregory. Michel was very much the jolly, round-faced Frenchman with his rather large spectacles and a broad grin which revealed a very full mouth of teeth. Gullivan noted that Michel was a complicated man, very much influenced by the philosophy of Nietzsche. His approach to philosophy was that of an anthropologist asking the question, how did the present come about, why do we believe what we now believe? Michel was rather quiet, reflective as if waiting for his turn to participate in the dinner table conversation.

Next to Michel was Claude Shannon. Claude was the epitome of the clean-cut, professional American scientist. He was fairly tall, lean to the point of gauntness. He impressed Gullivan as a listener, one who thinks carefully, calculates and then perhaps has something to say. His background was mathematics and electronics engineering and he was comfortable in his own competence. Indeed, one could claim that Claude was the father of information theory and the digital age. Rumor had it that Claude liked to juggle.

Ross Ashby, the quiet, rather serious British psychiatrist sat next to Claude. Ross was another complicated man and difficult to read. He sat back in his chair and seemed to be waiting for something. This quiet man-made enormous contributions to psychiatry with his "mathematical" representation of the brain and law of requisite variety. This law defines the minimum number of states necessary for a controller to control a system of a given number of states. Simply put for Gullivan's purposes, it takes variety to control variety.

Shunryu Suzuki, the Zen Master, sat next to the rather stern Ross. Shunryu looked quite different than the rest of the guests at the table and it wasn't just his lack of hair. He seemed to bring a sense of quiet peace, calm, and timeless wisdom to the table. Though born in Japan, he was influential in bringing Zen to the United States. Gullivan credited Shunryu for his understanding of the non-discussable reality of intuition and was very pleased he could come to the dinner party.

Frank, who sat next to Shunryu, was an artist and clearly enjoyed being seated next to the Zen Master. Frank is Polish/Irish with a round face and quite a twinkling eye. Gullivan would say of Frank that, if they both walked through Gullivan's garden, Frank would see much more than he. Frank knew Gordon, Humberto and Gregory very well and played a leading role in the "cybernetic" community. Gullivan often remembered the many long exploratory conversations he had with Frank, an artist's artist.

Gullivan's friend for many years, Paul, sat beside Frank. Paul had accompanied Gullivan on much of his journey and knew many of the guests. He was of medium height with a slim frame, a full head of dark hair; he radiated his Italian ancestry. He liked to play with computers, but was most at home on the piano or on stage. He was, like his tutor, Gordon, the consummate performer, quick with a smile or a song, but often very serious and profound.

Richard, the first or last of the guests, was, in a sense, an insider in the world of Macromol. Richard was Gullivan's mentor and took care of day to day details and messes so Gullivan could continue his quest. He was an upstate New Yorker of Germanic descent, tall, quiet, competent and a very good listener. Without Richard's wisdom, Gullivan doubted he would have had the opportunity to travel the world seeking answers to his questions.

When all had had their fill of food and wine, chairs were pushed back from the table and there was an air of anticipation. Frank began with a couple of related questions. "Where do problems come from?" Do we go in search of problems or do they find us?" He recalled a meeting he had had with his art students and Gullivan. They discussed the question "do people decide to become artists or does art draw them in?" Frank answered that somehow "art" draws in the artist. Gregory noted that this was an important point because if you think you make decisions, it leads you in a certain direction, perhaps the end of personal reflection. On the other hand, Gregory said if you see what you did, what you decided, as a description of yourself at that time, then self-knowledge could be enhanced.

Richard pointed out that many at the table, let's call them the teachers or the theoreticians, have posed formidable problems to themselves. Erwin asked, what is the quantum mechanical structure of the hydrogen atom? Gordon asked, what is the nature of human conversation? Humberto asked, what is life, a living system? Ross asked, what properties must a system have in order to function like a brain, to learn to adapt for the better? Gregory asked, what is the link between person to person, person to group, and group to wider social order communication? Michel asked, how does the now truth come to be and how is it manifest? Claude asked, how do we accurately and efficiently send messages over transmission systems? And perhaps Shunryu asked the age-old question, how do I find the ultimate truth?

The other guests might be said to have been students of these teachers who have learned from their extraordinary work and are now trying to apply these learnings to every day concerns. Shunryu said that perhaps many of the teachers had gone through a process similar to that which he went through as a student in a Zen monastery. It was there he was given a koan, a problem that could not be solved using the conventional thinking of the day. Only when the logical thinking mind grew frustrated and exhausted over this problem, did the problem change its nature. It became a problem of intuitively knowing, rather than logically deducing. Remember how Einstein "became" the beam of light in order to see that the ether problem was no problem at all – the speed of light was constant. It was an intuitive moment.

Building on this, Paul said that Gullivan had found himself with a problem of a similar nature. Why were so many bad investments being made in Macromol? Why were scarce resources of human talent and capital being devoted to technologies of the past, while the technological world around them was changing so fast? Erwin agreed and said there were really two problems. First, what was the nature of a good investment – what necessary and sufficient conditions would qualify it as such? And secondly, how do we recognize it and discuss it?

Gordon suggested that we discuss these two problems separately. The first can be discussed using the language of science, what one might call the rational domain. The second problem is more problematic since, if the technology were new to Macromol, how could it be discussed by the Cardinals who knew little about it?

Erwin said he found himself in agreement with Gullivan in turning to thermodynamics to find a sound basis for exploring the first question about what constitutes a good investment. He said that with respect to order and disorder he was sure that the sciences of thermodynamics (dealing with heat, energy and entropy), of biology (dealing with living systems) and of economics (mathematical descriptions of human behavior in terms of money, goods, services and value) were all viewpoints of the same reality. Burning coal generates heat to warm ourselves, but creates disorder by doing so. The chicken pecks at specks of food strewn around the barnyard enabling it to grow and ultimately to lay an egg – order from disorder through structure. On the economic side, we organize bricks to build a house or words to author a book.

Then Michel said that when we look at this from an historical perspective, we can see where problems can arise, where the simplicity is lost. The engineers, the biologists and the economists each have their own history, their own concerns, self-interests and manner of making a living. Thus, in an evolutionary sense, it is not surprising that they can no longer discuss the same thing at the simple level of order and disorder. They have evolved apart from having different species of language. Perhaps we shall return to this difficulty later.

Erwin said that Gullivan's answer to the nature of a good investment question is what he calls economic potential – a simple number equal to the value of the output less the lowest cost of the input divided by the latter. In other words, if we take an abundant input like sand and combine it with the addition of other trace elements, we can make something of great value, namely silicon chips, the foundation of modern information computation and communication technology. As Gullivan mentioned earlier in his story, when Carver Mead asked how many functions can be put on a given area of silicon, based on the laws of physics, some bright people saw the vast potential in the new technology which was just beginning.

Richard said we had a similar case in Macromol. With the invention
of organic macromolecules in the early part of the twentieth century, a
perceptive Cardinal in Macromol asked, "Why can't we make strong string,
perhaps to replace wool?" Thus began the great age of macromolecular
chemistry around the world.

Claude reminded the guests that Gullivan has derived an economic potential
number of about 20 for the strong string. He also noted that the journey
of realizing the inherent potential involved taking the ignorance out of the
system, finding out how to reduce the cost, reinvest, lower price and thus
expand. When the economic potential was exhausted (when the number was
close to one), the input costs were about half the output value. There was,
except in the case of a monopoly, no good reason to invest either in research,
as there was nothing else to ask, or in new production facilities, as there was
little return on that investment. But, said Claude, something very interesting
happened along the path to greater and greater efficiency. I see how Gullivan
used the same understanding of the relative frequency of letters, words and
phrases in the English language as I used in my work on information theory.
However, Gullivan came at it in a different way. He looked at what happened
to the language of the social system as the machines became more efficient.
The language narrowed in focus, shorthand was adopted, and errors in
instructions declined as essentially the same messages were transmitted over
and over again. People knew what they were doing, they were not confused.
This path to efficiency, although it has obvious economic benefits, is also
the path to the reduction of plasticity in the language. As time went by,
new technologies, new concepts, word possibilities were evolving outside of
Macromol. How could, and perhaps why should, these new outside ideas be
discussed inside the narrowly evolved Macromol?

What we now need to explore is how to succeed in changing the regime of
the truth in a multi-generational island which was previously very successful,
but whose survival is now being threatened by evolutionary changes in the
world outside of it. Can we indeed change so we can have, as Gullivan said,

conservation of capital and not creative destruction with all of its pain and displacement. Gullivan remarked that Humberto told him that in order to see what can be changed, we must first look at what is conserved – biological systems are very conservative, as Humberto has noted.

As we know, Paul said, Gullivan borrowed Ross's *Design for a Brain* work and modified it to address not the personal single brain problem, but the interpersonal or multi-brain problem, a subject of great interest to Gregory, who has written much on this subject.

Gregory chimed in, yes, I understand the direction Gullivan took and how it suited his purpose. Indeed, social systems over time conserve certain beliefs and ideals – for example, the role of the constitution I the United States. I was quite interested in how Gullivan went from Ross's work to his own construct of Macromol as a social system. In Ross's description, essential variables are those whose values are conserved between upper and lower limits, like glucose levels and blood pressure in the human body. The single brain system learns through the double-loop system of trial and error which Gullivan described earlier. In Gullivan's view, the essential variables in social organizations are shared truths held within the organization. Among these were the hierarchical nature of Macromol, similar to the Catholic church, the imperative to project a positive future outlook to the market and maintain the rituals that sustained these variables. For the individual in Macromol, the essential social variables were those that pertained to social status, identity, the manner of making a living and, in general, personal social security or the feeling that I am safe. So returning to Ross's work on what it is to learn: How can the people in Macromol learn, by trial and error, with new ideas and concepts from outside Macromol? How can the knowledgeable individual risk his livelihood to initiate discussions that reveal that the current truth in Macromol is faulty?

This, I believe, is where it gets interesting, said Humberto, who had been quietly listening. We have discussed what is conserved and cannot change without substantial dislocation to all of Macromol. We have also alluded to the fact that the new truth, the new concepts, ideas and language, exist outside of Macromol. Let us look at Macromol as a social system: the relevant environment is the historically evolved and agreed-upon system of values, beliefs, social structures, norms and rituals in language. The medium of behavior in social systems including Macromol is language rather than anything physical, because language is the medium of the agreements, instructions and transactions that constitute the forward motion (discuss, agree, invest) within Macromol in its own terms. Humberto went on to state that the area of possible change requires us to look at what can be discussed. How can changes in language around what can be discussed be brought about without the players losing their heads?

Humberto continued, we accept Gullivan's notion of invention as the opening of new semantic spaces, and the nature of its occurrence as rare and perhaps somewhat random. We also know that these occurrences are preceded by a koan, like the experiences to which Shunryu alluded to. After years of concentration and consternation with conventional thinking, finally (Eureka!) an intuitive grasp of the new truth reveals itself. This being so, how can we expect the Prince to grasp the new truth? I agree with Gullivan that we must introduce a new speaker, one who understands the power and utility of the invention, the new semantic space. Yet the speaker must have the talent to convey this new truth to others, that is, to bring a new language into being. So how do we recognize this new speaker, that Gullivan calls the Queen, the mother of the new language? How is the Queen successfully introduced to the court at Macromol, and, in Michel's language, by what design does she change the regime of truth?

It seems to me said Humberto that regenerative change by design is simple biology: conception through mixing of existing languages, birth, and development. It should be noted, however, that speciation, in the body or in language, requires a separation or distance so "adaptation" (development of new language) can occur.

I think, said Erwin, that we are all pretty much in agreement, but is the queen a person, or perhaps a group that has the requisite variety to accomplish the task?

Assuming, said Claude, that we have fortunately found a suitable Queen, I think we would all agree that it is absolutely imperative that she picks the right problem – one that draws on the new semantic spaces in communication, computation, biological and materials technologies. Gullivan has already outlined some of the characteristics of the focusing problem including the political, such that the requirements of distance can be met.

As the dinner guests converged on the possibility of change by design, Gregory stood up and said, what is said is not what is heard. The political issue may not be the message itself, but whether the message can be heard at a particular time. The listener could be limited in language variety to actually hear and understand the message.

Shunryu raised his hand and said perhaps there is another difficulty which underlies Gullivan's whole story. In our practice, as I have said, we give the student a problem, commonly referred to as a koan. The purpose of this problem is to bring about a fundamental change in the student's experience of seeing into his own Nature. The student uses the logic of Plato in the beginning, but after a long process of concentration, confusion and analysis, he reaches a block. At this point a spark sometimes occurs and the student intuitively experiences his true Nature. My point is that the conventional world of logic, calculations, analysis, thinking, language and its dualistic nature has its uses, but it is not the experience of intuition or direct knowing. The intuitive inventor always faces the problem of explaining his experiences, such as the solution to a problem or the dissolution of a dilemma, to those who experience their own world in conventional language. Those, the Prince among them, might ask how could the intuitor see the whole answer, why is he convinced he has the "right" answer.

I'm sure that Frank has experienced "being in the painting," where the brush appears to move by itself guided perhaps by intuition. Contrast that with the next day experience of looking at what happened. The writer experiences the feeling that the pen moves by its own accord. My point is the intuitive experience is outside language. The gulf between language, logic and its dualistic nature, and the oneness or unity of the intuitive experience. How does one describe the beauty of the rose? The Queen has to be comfortable in both experiences, the intuitive and the conventional dualistic world.

Gullivan, Paul, Richard and Frank went outside and sat around the table on the flagstone patio just outside the dining room. The journey for me, Gullivan said, started many years ago, with the questions – what constitutes a good investment, how does it come into the course of events, and how is it born, take hold and thrive? I believe we have answered these questions. Richard and I, acting as the Queen, articulated a legitimate focusing problem. The specified problem met all the requirements of economic potential, evolutionary current in that the mode of productivity was based on replacing mass and energy (stuff) with information. The solution was potentially generative, surplus could be reinvested to create further surplus, and indeed that process could be replicated. Richard and Gullivan, over the course of a year, brought the project to the point of validating the assumptions made about market value, costs, engineering principles and requirements, and indeed the basic model of the required transaction communication, production, shipment, and financial considerations.

The time came then for Richard and the Jester to get the financial backing and support to give birth to this new form of activity in Macromol. They met with Cardinal Chance. The process would either go forward or die, depending on how Cardinal Chance could hear the proposal, and on whether or not he could align what he might hear with his self-interest. The outcome was indeed disappointing for Richard and the Jester. However, should one be surprised? Cardinal Chance, with his many years in Macromol and his obedience to the perceived wishes of the Prince, could indeed not hear what Richard and the Jester had to say. He did not understand the language, he had not lived in that world, and he was focused on current activities and the next quarter's financial results – indeed, conserving what he already believed.

There is much talk of change, change for the better. It is politically popular and the speakers revel in their performances. However, in previously successful social systems, change by design will not occur except through the careful work described above and good fortune. I wonder, Gullivan said, what the conversations in Macromol might be today if the focusing problem, the new direction in investing was given life.

The Dinner Party – an alternative ending

Gullivan posed the question, on a second or third generation island, how do we recognize and select the Queen, such that we facilitate the creative conservation of capital, avoiding the misery that comes with the destruction of capital? Through the natural deselection process? Gullivan noted that on first and perhaps second-generation islands, there is usually sufficient creation of new distinctions, new language to complete the Red Phase. Hence the question is how to start a viable Red Phase as the island moves further into the Blue Phase.

Humberto said, this is indeed a difficult problem, inasmuch as biology is very conservative and the drive to conserve the prevailing world view, truth, essential variables in a social system like the island of Macromol, which has been from an evolutionary point of view very successful, the conservative forces in language, behavior are very strong.

Gordon said that we have conversations with ourselves, perhaps over many selves, and of course with others, and in the course of our journey, we have acquired beliefs, ways of simplifying, collapsing complexity, and these we enact and give or make meaning in our ongoing lives. Therefore, for a person successfully placed in the Blue Phase to give birth to or even understand a new Red Phase would require that such a person have an entirely new conversation with herself. Now how could this happen, the necessary variety of concepts and directions in language are not on the "island" of such a person. They do not know that they do not know.

This reminds me of a koan, Shunryu said, so we need to feel the answer, become this embodied Queen, empty the mind, meditate and let the answer arise in a manner similar to Einstein's path.

Perhaps so, said Gregory, we indeed, as Gordon said, would have to change our existing encoding and meaning making system, we would, as Shunryu said, have to suspend or at least examine the now validity of what we hold to be true. Normally we accomplish this by insight, frustration, the koan, though sometimes events or conversations occur which change us to the core. Now

Gullivan talked to many teachers, are we the right people to answer the question? We are all theoreticians, inventors of new distinctions, but we are talking about the Queen, the one who makes things happen in the world. We are once again dealing with the law of requisite variety. Do we have the necessary conceptual and perhaps emotional variety to fully answer the question? After all, none of us has nursed a "business" from conception to independent life. However, perhaps we can point the way to the required variety to satisfactorily answer the question.

Claude said, I was very interested in Gullivan's understanding of the consequences of efficiency in a social system. As you know, I was primarily interested in sending messages, regardless of their meaning, over wires, the telephone system, but I can see the relationship between efficiency, decreasing plasticity and thus the danger of extinction. It would seem to me that one should have the Queen in place in the green phase as the downside to efficiency begins to manifest itself.

In my language, Michel said, we are discussing change in the regime of the truth. This, of course, occurs naturally every day, as Shunryu would tell us. The cosmos, the world, we change from microsecond to microsecond. The task is, how do we bring about a new truth, new language, and a new regime of truth by design. This, in France, we would think of as a problem of seduction.

Now all this time the Jester was in the mirror and finally spoke. The Queen must not be a member of the now social system. She should perhaps be a Jester. This we understand both from the biology of speciation and the creative destruction of capital. So perhaps the Queen, be she singular or plural, requires a function to find her, in Ross's language. Perhaps there is a process. We start with a search team, let them discuss the limits of their own variety and learn, as Ashby notes, by trial and error, by focused discussions until they reach the Aha! moment – enlightenment, yes we intuitively know we can do this. Of course, the team players are not members of Macromol and can be said as a team to have the variety necessary to articulate and discuss the evolutionary current new semantic spaces, concepts and inventions.

Foucault said, I think it is important to reflect on the nature of truth and power, and who is not the Queen. The Cardinals, courtiers and perhaps others might, in their lack of awareness of their own limitations and ignorance, convince themselves that they can perform the function of the Queen. Indeed, inventors of semantic space, like most of us here, are not Queen. The Queen is apolitical, driven to create new social spaces through the recognition of what is now possible. The main source of error is in misunderstanding who is not the Queen, and the need for mental, emotional, political and physical separation from the Blue inhabitants.

Richard noted that he had many experiences of the court, the presumption of power, when the court blocked, dismissed many attempts to regenerate life in Macromol. They had become addicted to the drive for efficiency. Now perhaps the lessons learned suggest that the Queen's authority should come not from the Prince but from the Board – those responsible, in principle, for the survival of the island. The Prince cannot hear.

So Gullivan said it seems that the first task is to guess at a team with the appropriate skills, to begin the discussion in which the team reveals its own limitations, and then, through trial and error, become convinced that they are ready to "design" the function of the Queen. Gullivan had been through such a process in the early 1980's, trying to conceptualize the world of intelligent material systems. The meeting with the group of scientists, engineers, biologists, system thinkers, and mathematicians, was most instructive. Over the first two days, each member spoke from his perspective, and then there was a sense of unease, quiet frustration thinking we had hit the wall – a koan. The next day, conversation began to quicken and amazing insights began to pour out. I remember that experience well, said Gullivan, and I think if you don't experience "hitting the wall" and go through that phase, little change will occur.

www.ingramcontent.com/pod-product-compliance
Lightning Source LLC
Chambersburg PA
CBHW032019170526
45157CB00002B/775